PRAISE FOR
MAKE YOUR MOMENT

"Loads of practical advice all of us can use. Pick and choose what suits you and your personality. And enjoy reading this engaging book!"

—CONNIE CHUNG, television journalist

"Dion is a trailblazer whose spirit is undeniably radiant. She illuminates a room with infectious energy! Dion is a champion for women and has followed her passion, which transcends every time she is on the screen and now in her fantastic new book!"

—JACKIE SORKIN, entrepreneur, founder of Candytopia, and Candy Queen

"Dion Lim shows us why people love her. With inimitable everywoman storytelling, she shares her amazing journey from insecure cub reporter to assured anchorwoman. Men should read it to understand how much harder the road is for women. Women should read it to know they are not alone as well as to benefit from Dion's hard-won, savvy social intelligence insights and communication tips."

—DION LIM [not related], former COO of Simply Hired and current CEO of NextLesson

"Dion Lim is a savvy, good-hearted woman with a record that proves she knows what it takes to survive and thrive in work and life. She knows what it takes to Make Your Moment because she's done it."

—DAN RATHER, television journalist

"Pursuing a dream—Olympic or otherwise—takes perseverance and determination. Victory is sweet but never in the absence of obstacles and challenges. How do we navigate them? So many great anecdotal situations from Dion to lend perspective and insight. A fun and informative read!"

—Kristi Yamaguchi, Olympic
champion figure skater

"Dion's book is like having a brutally honest, funny, and wise best friend by your side during your most stressed and drama-filled times at work. No matter what you do or where you want to take your career you'll relate to the stories in this book and be ready for whatever comes your way.

"Whether you're just graduating from college or a seasoned professional, this book is a must for women! Dion's got a refreshing candor and realness that resonates with everybody and her advice is guaranteed to help you conquer your career."

—Tiffany Amber Thiessen,
actress and author of *Pull Up a Chair*

"Dion's communications playbook is brimming with wise and practical lessons and perspectives told in a very authentic and compelling manner. Her willingness to transparently share her personal experiences, lessons, challenges, and triumphs are valuable and transformative no matter what your background or where you are in your personal journey. I love it! People will really benefit not only from reading it but practicing it!"

—Mary Stutts, Chief Inclusion,
Diversity & Health Equity Officer, Stanford
Health Care, and author of *The Missing Mentor*

"Working for my 150 year-old family-owned and operated chocolate company, I know how important communication is to inspiring and maintaining workplace harmony. Whether you read *Make Your Moment* cover to cover or dive in one chapter here and there, Dion provides genuine guidance that builds a level of confidence for you to handle whatever comes your way, even if it's your own inner dialogue. A tool for any leader's toolbox."

—AMY GUITTARD, Director of Marketing at Guittard Chocolate Company

"What Dion Lim learned in the high-pressure, sometimes-backstabbing world of broadcast news could serve budding professionals well as they seek to build their career—no matter their industry. The workplace wisdom Dion Lim shares through confessional anecdotes is exactly what young professionals need to better navigate the sometimes thorny relationships that exist among colleagues."

—JENNIFER COOGAN, the Chief Content Officer for Newsela

make
— YOUR —
moment

THE SAVVY WOMAN'S
COMMUNICATION
PLAYBOOK FOR
GETTING THE SUCCESS
YOU WANT

DION LIM

Mc Graw Hill

NEW YORK   CHICAGO   SAN FRANCISCO   ATHENS   LONDON   MADRID   MEXICO CITY
MILAN   NEW DELHI   SINGAPORE   SYDNEY   TORONTO

1 2 3 4 5 6 7 8 9   QVS   24 23 22 21 20 19

ISBN: 978-1-260-45546-5
MHID: 1-260-45546-7

e-ISBN: 978-1-260-45547-2
e-MHID: 1-260-45547-5

Design by Lee Fukui and Mauna Eichner

Library of Congress Cataloging-in-Publication Data

Names: Lim, Dion, author.
Title: Make your moment : the savvy woman's communication playbook for getting the success you want / Dion Lim.
Description: New York : McGraw-Hill, [2020] | Includes bibliographical references and index.
Identifiers: LCCN 2019028625 (print) | LCCN 2019028626 (ebook) | ISBN 9781260455465 (hardcover) | ISBN 9781260455472 (ebook)
Subjects: LCSH: Women—Vocational guidance. | Communication in management. | Career development. | Success in business.
Classification: LCC HF5382.6 .L56 2019 (print) | LCC HF5382.6 (ebook) | DDC 650.101/4—dc23
LC record available at https://lccn.loc.gov/2019028625
LC ebook record available at https://lccn.loc.gov/2019028626

McGraw-Hill Education books are available at special quantity discounts to use as premiums and sales promotions or for use in corporate training programs. To contact a representative, please visit the Contact Us pages at www.mhprofessional.com.

*To everyone who believed in me
before I believed in myself.*

Contents

Acknowledgments
ix

Introduction
The Communication Playbook
xi

1

Reacting 101
Sounds Basic, but It's *Everything*
1

2

The Interpersonal Battlefield
Navigating the Awkward, the Unexpected,
the Downright Bizarre
25

3

The Betta Fish
Lessons from the Workplace Fish Tank
47

4

The Matt Lauer Effect
Intelligent Courage
77

CONTENTS

5

Survival Speak

Talking Your Way Through the Daily Minefield

97

6

More Than a Pickup Artist

Connect and Keep Up with Anyone and Everyone

143

7

Talk to the Voices in Your Head

Communicate with Yourself First, in
Order to Communicate with Others

161

8

Optics

What's on the Outside Matters More Than You Think

187

9

Fail Your Way Forward

Sometimes It Takes One Step Back to
Bound Light-Years Forward

199

Epilogue

227

Index

229

Acknowledgments

As someone who writes two-minute stories and reads on TV for a living, writing a book was completely out of my comfort zone. I had no idea how the process worked or how challenging it would be. (Wait, I need to use complete sentences?)

This book would not have happened without some pretty remarkable people: To my friend Sara, for encouraging me five years ago to make a seemingly impossible goal of writing a book a reality. To my phenomenal literary agent, Lilly, for her unwavering support from the day she read my disjointed, pathetic excuse of a proposal and has gone above and beyond in championing me every step of the way. To my editorial director at McGraw-Hill, Donya, who saw our vision, shared my passion, and ran with it. To my husband, who kept me sane and held down the fort while I tapped away at paragraphs here and there while traipsing around the country covering natural disasters, NBA celebrations, the Oscars, and anything else in-between. To my parents, for being terrible communicators but who inspired me through their hard work to become what they couldn't. To my viewers across the country, many of whom have followed me on this wild journey no matter what city. Oh, and to the many coffee shops (Blue Bottle, in particular) in San Francisco that didn't mind me posting up for hours, monopolizing precious cafe table real estate to get this book done.

Introduction
The Communication Playbook

For three years, my jaw didn't work correctly. Eating anything that required opening my mouth more than two inches (sandwiches, apples, and corn on the cob were all out of the question) resulted in my mandible popping out of place and painfully dislocating. Forget about watching sporting events. I'd forget about this little issue while wildly cheering for the home team after a nearly impossible three-pointer and my jaw would painfully remind me to take the enthusiasm down a notch to a six-inch voice.

This was a direct result of my job. No question about it. Not convenient for someone who talks—a lot—for a living. What was really going on behind the poised, well-spoken, thousand-watt Crest Whitestrips–smile and shellacked anchor hair, was a stressed, anxiety-filled, insecure woman in her early twenties who grinded her teeth subconsciously at night as if to pulverize all her problems away. Even though I was working the morning shift, waking up at 3 a.m. and dead tired by 4 p.m., most nights were spent staring at the ceiling, thinking about the troubles and drama of the day, playing over and over again on an endless loop. The co-anchor, twice my age, wouldn't talk to me in the commercial break but would pretend to be my friend when the red on-air light was flicked on for tens of thousands of people. I had to continually extract myself gracefully from Eddy, the administrative assistant who talked my ear off while I tried to get work done. (And even worse, all while staring at my boobs.) How could someone supposedly be so well-liked by viewers to be named "best morning anchor" by the local newspaper, yet go home in tears nearly every day feeling like a nobody because of the awkward/difficult/emotionally charged conversations that took place inside the office? Or how, being the new kid at work, 15 years younger than everyone else, makes me a prime target for jealousy, trash-talk, and drama. Or that I'd be that person at a networking mixer hiding in a bathroom stall, petrified. Neither school nor industry conferences had prepared me for the reality of an office and the daily interpersonal challenges I had to face. You may know the feeling. If you work with people (and who doesn't?), you've probably found yourself in intense office settings trying to figure out how to navigate situations you never dreamed of encountering.

It took four moves across the country, working as the first and only full-time Asian American anchor in three different markets in an incredibly competitive, often cruel industry to finally figure out what was wrong. In the business of communication, I was communicating all wrong! On the air, I could make magic. Not only did I have a knack for convincing reluctant people to go on camera and talk to me, they often spilled their guts, pouring out their hearts, and telling me everything about their lives, just short of their bank account numbers. Even an entire auditorium full of rowdy, puberty-stricken, angsty teens at my public appearances would sit still and listen as I made a story come to life. Yet in the office, I couldn't get the attention and respect I knew I deserved.

It turns out the intangible skills I honed out in the world as a reporter made for an excellent training ground in mastering the micro interactions of the workplace and in my career. Interacting with everyone from suspected child molesters to rural farmworkers and Hollywood starlets, coupled with the inherent talent of growing up and dealing with a Chinese Tiger Mom and dad who culturally didn't know how to communicate with their very Americanized daughter, prepared me for almost everything that came my way.

It just took me a long time to figure it all out. And in this book, I hope to share all my hard-earned lessons with you.

Your workplace may be an interpersonal battlefield and it's likely not getting any less complicated. Along with competition and predatory behavior, there's a new online dynamic to contend with as well. Status updates and ideas spread at the speed of light on Facebook, Twitter, Instagram, and what seems like a new social network that pops up every other week. But so does the hate, judgment, negativity, and all the behaviors that rear their ugly heads out from behind a computer screen.

Take Carol, who always tattles about your workplace performance to the boss because she wants your job. Or, the room full of high-powered doctors or executives at an end-of-year work party you want to rub elbows with, but are too intimidated to even approach. Then there's finding a way to gracefully recover from totally flubbing a lecture in front of three dozen colleagues because your PowerPoint presentation crashed. We haven't even gotten to the World Wide Web yet either, where it takes just seconds for someone to Google your name and a few more to spew out some nasty trolling remarks meant to hurt your feelings and get in the way of your success.

How are you supposed to move up the ladder, when all of these factors are trying to keep you down?

As women, I know we're constantly being told to "speak up," "lean in," and be a "badass," and to go "unf**k" ourselves and represent the hashtag #MeToo movement. We absolutely should. We must! But we have to execute these things in the right way. Here's a secret: you don't have to be the most talented, the smartest, the most attractive, or even the most skilled person at your job to get what you want out of your career and in life. I'm definitely not any of those, and have a very mediocre SAT score, C chemistry grades, and remedial math classes to prove that! (Being promoted at almost every job I've had has nothing to do with knowing the square root of pi.)

So, let's do it better. In this book, you'll learn the hard-earned skills of mastering communication with the world and with yourself. With the tools I provide you, you'll be able to tackle it all. Whether you're fresh out of college, accepting your first job at a law firm, or a seasoned manager ready for a new career breakthrough, you'll learn how to master the basic interactions nobody taught you in corporate training—or even talks about, *period*. You'll learn that these "micro" interactions are what actually build our reputations and credibility and ultimately shape our careers. Each chapter will take you through one of the most common workplace challenges and show you how to use communication to successfully navigate that challenge. The right kind of communication will create new opportunities, empower you, and give you the self-assuredness needed to accomplish whatever your goals are in your career—all without years of having to wear a dorky dental night guard like I did.

So, are you ready? Let's dive in!

Reacting 101
Sounds Basic, but It's
Everything

*Y*EAH, YEAH. We've all heard the sayings about reactions to events: Loose lips sink ships! Think before you speak! Never let them see you cry/sweat! I am woman, hear me roar! To some extent, these things are true. It's probably not a good idea to talk about your manager's foul egg-salad body odor to his assistant. Or to call out the IT guy as a creeper when he holds your hand in a handshake a little too long. But we'll get to that part later.

Ladies, you already know this.

But what we don't realize is that every encounter we have in the workplace is like a performance review . . . and that review may not come from our bosses, but from our peers and those who are watching these interactions happen. We are constantly being judged on our abilities to get along with others and be trustworthy and valuable to the organization. The magic of communicating to get the success you want starts with identifying the reactions of others, so you can properly respond yourself. Because half the battle in staying alive (we can talk about thriving after we've figured out how to just survive) in a workplace chock-full of people with varying opinions, skill levels, and backgrounds is learning how to react to the odd, awkward, and downright crappy situations and interactions that may come your way.

UH, EXCUSE ME: WHAT DID YOU JUST SAY? (HOW TO DEAL)

As I was growing up in a traditional Chinese household, my parents taught me it was best to avoid ruffling feathers in the face of adversity. I think this came from their early years in the United States, when they feared being deported. They would tell me cliffhanger stories of their first few years living in Texas before I was born and how neighbors would throw eggs at their windows and call out to them using racial slurs. I'd beg, "Then what happened, ma?" which almost always resulted in an anticlimactic response of, "Nothing." And it was on to the next topic. In their eyes, keeping my head down, working hard, and doing my best would always yield success! As a chemist, my dad was the perfect bookworm in school who studied hard and then regularly worked 12-hour days to advance in his career. This was just how they were brought up and how they chose to define their path to workplace triumph.

While this was perfectly fine for my parents and perhaps those of their generation, the pendulum swings far the other way for women today. We're constantly being told to "speak up!" and firmly beat our chests to be heard. "Hear me roar!" Be your baddest badass bitch! (Aren't you sick of these affirmation T-shirts yet?)

Unfortunately, even though this is the message we're receiving, speaking our mind doesn't always fly in the workplace.

When I started working, it took a long time for me to learn how to stand up for myself in the right way. At first, I didn't think I had a right to protest or fire back because of my age and (lack of) experience level. When I did become experienced enough where I felt like I could respond, I went to the opposite extreme and was unnecessarily combative.

There were so many inappropriate, awkward interactions, and I had no idea how to be ready for them. There was the client who insults Greek people ("They all smell like feta cheese!") not knowing my husband is Greek. The boss who asked me to compromise my ethics and exaggerate numbers and figures from a research document. And my favorite: the on-air coworker who was shamed after gaining several pounds when a manager accused her of carrying twins. All true stories.

I quickly learned that it wasn't actually about having the biggest voice, but rather having the right one. Whether it's by sassing someone back, getting creative in how to gradually nudge a coworker, or sometimes by being still and doing nothing, there's a way to handle these situations where you don't compromise your own ethics, values, and beliefs or get labeled a combative, raging maniac. There is a way to react to situations where you can feel totally in control.

REACTIONS: USE YOUR EMOTIONS THE RIGHT WAY

Let's be honest. The idea of being "controlled" or trying to "control" anything doesn't sound fun. Nothing is more abhorrent than a controlling significant other who doesn't allow you to go out with your friends on a Friday night. Or a controlling parent who won't let you go outside and play but instead forces you to stay inside, plinking away at piano keys for hours until you perform the sonata by memory. (I speak from experience on that one.) Or even the self-control to not eat the entire block of aged Irish cheddar, even though you know how good it tastes. This is why I detest the idea of controlling your reactions and emotions, which is the advice my parents doled out when I tried to talk to them about workplace issues. "Ay-yahhhh. Didi, just control your anger! It's that easy!" my dad would smile. That never worked. Instead, I think of it as training yourself to have the discipline to use your reactions correctly. Because when you do, some pretty powerful things can happen. It all starts with understanding the potential in a reaction.

The Power of a Reaction: In storytelling, the magic, the hook, the most compelling part is in the reaction. The joy on a little boy's face when his father comes home from deployment. The shock of a new mom and dad to be discovering they're having triplets. This happens in the news world all the time. Ever notice how the camera always zooms in on someone crying or laughing hysterically? I once had a producer who would, in all seriousness, ask the team after we came back from a day of shooting in the field, "Did you make tears flow today?" in a half-joking-yet-not-joking-insensitive way. Simply said: reactions have power. Choosing how to use your first reaction is the beginning step in effectively getting what you want.

While reactions in the workplace may not be as emotionally charged as the examples I just gave, recognizing others' reactions and calibrating yours can be the difference between landing a big contract, getting a "no" and not making your monthly quota, or winning the support of a higher-up who has never noticed you before.

Adjust Emotionally: Act and React Like the Pro You Are

Years ago, a news manager who was trying to get me to sign another contract at the television station with no raise told me I would never be able to land a job as good as the one I had. In hindsight, this manager's intentions weren't to be cruel. He just really wanted me to stay at the station and get away with not paying me the raise I should have gotten in order to stay. But in the shock and anger of the moment, without thinking, I started sobbing. How dare he devalue my skills and say I wasn't skilled enough or talented enough, or *anything* enough to find a higher-ranking position that paid more than my current salary?

My rage and disappointment were so strong, they didn't brew inside me. They exploded. In-between ugly, guttural sobs, I went off the rails, ranting how, actually, stations across the country had already expressed interest in having me come in for an interview. Bigger ones that paid much more. The result of this Niagara Falls of a reaction? The manager ended up calling my agent shortly afterward to inform him an ultimatum was in place. Either renew my contract at a flat pay or leave.

In hindsight, that experience was a disaster. Deep down, I didn't want to stay because I was hitting a professional wall and not growing. There was no challenge to the work. Knowing there were more lucrative jobs available on the horizon meant I had an opportunity to explore new options. But my explosive, messy, snotty-nosed response just escalated the situation and caused me to divulge secrets about my job search and sent an ugly message to my boss that I was not the leader he thought I was.

But there *was* a leader within me. It just happened to get bogged down by the emotional gut-punch. There's a leader within you, too—it just needs to be unleashed. Read on for your 101 on how to turn that seemingly devastating/unexpected/upsetting encounter around to make your moment.

Train Your Brain to Wait a Minute . . . or Maybe 1,440 (Prevent the Knee-Jerk)

As a reporter, the knee-jerk reaction is usually the best video and sound bite you'll get. It's the response immediately after something wonderful/violent/unjust happens. How can we not be transfixed by intoxicated and elated Philadelphia Eagles fans climbing greased telephone poles after winning the Super Bowl? Or be captivated by a young woman who discovers she has a long-lost twin after taking one of those at-home DNA tests?

But the problem with reacting without thinking in the workplace is that your emotions aren't fully processed and fleshed out, so they may not be accurate. Rioters who are protesting the minimum wage certainly aren't thinking through why they're setting a car on fire or thinking about the consequences of doing it. Instead, their pent-up frustrations at the government brim over into violent, angry acts when there are other ways to take a stand and get your voice heard with a little thinking and brainstorming. It's only *after* they get arrested and charged with disorderly conduct that they realize their spur-of-the-moment reactions didn't serve them so well.

The same applies to the workplace.

When I get an email that infuriates or frustrates me, I never respond right away, or even an hour later. Instead, I'll give myself the satisfaction of typing out my initial response but not pressing send. By waiting a full day, I let the true meaning of what happened that prompted the email sink in and process. After waiting

1,440 minutes, I revisit the email and 100 percent of the time, I never send the first draft. Allowing the emotion to temper with a bit of time usually results in a response that's a more thought-out and intelligent reaction that can lead to a solution instead of creating a bigger problem. (You'll read about my own professional, or should I say unprofessional email flop later.)

When it comes to real-life conversations, you may not always be able to wait a full day, or even five minutes, to respond. But you can at least take a breath, excuse yourself temporarily (there is no shame in admitting that the three caramel lattes you had before work necessitate an immediate trip to the restroom), or ask to revisit the subject at a later time. In hindsight, I should have suggested my boss talk about money directly to my agent and politely excused myself from the conversation.

Practice conscious pausing. Doing so will eventually become second-nature and you'll find your responses more fully developed and appropriate for the situation at hand.

USE EMOTIONALLY CHARGED REACTIONS TO YOUR ADVANTAGE

Every business professional, mentor, or friend will tell you not to cry at work under any circumstances. But I'm a crier. As a child my mother told me Chinese girls weren't supposed to cry unless their mother dies. My mom's harsh approach had the opposite effect—I started crying at everything, even a papercut. But later on, after the botched contract-renewing conversation, I discovered by accident that whenever I was upset or unhappy with someone's actions or words, a slight show of sentiment could hammer home my point more effectively than if I were to deliver my response stone-faced.

Allowing just a tiny prickle of tears to form behind my eyes but not quite fall conveys the seriousness of a situation, or how hurt I am without having to go into full-on snotty-nosed "where's my tissue" weepy mode. Before you label me as manipulative, hear me out. I'm showing genuine passion and feelings, not trying to deceive or put on a facade. When you're truly frustrated, angry, or upset, tears may be your actual response. They're just adjusted down to the point where your message can be heard loud and clear and not caught up in the fog of a full-on sob session.

It's also not just the tears that can be effective. Kind of how growing up my mom—and probably your parents, too—would give me a look that said, "Didi, you in *big* trouble!" With a slight frown or furrow of a brow, you can show disappointment and can send a signal to the other person that you're not pleased without having to say anything at all.

In the end, what the manager did was not effective on many levels. He should not have talked to me about finances in that manner, and instead of using a negative (me not being able to find a "better" job), he would have been more successful with some positive reinforcement and encouragement to stay. "Dion, your recognition score is high, and we appreciate your hard work. We'd really like you to stay on for many years."

Oh, and in case you're wondering, I did get a job better than the one I had. A larger market, that paid almost double.

TALKING BODIES: THE SUBTLE VISUAL CLUES THAT GET YOU WHAT YOU WANT

News Flash: The words that come from someone else's mouth are just a small indication of how they're really feeling. Just like the watering of the eyes I mentioned in the previous section, there's a lot that can be told from a person's tiny, sometimes nearly undetectable body language. You just need to know how to look out for it.

Watch the Eyes

Watching someone's eyes is one of the most crucial ways to learn how to react. Notice subtle cues like eyes drifting, shifting, or glazing over. Whenever this happens, I know whatever I'm saying is not interesting and it's my job to either (1) present the content in a more riveting fashion (because what's the point of continuing if someone's zoning out and not absorbing what you're saying) or (2) it's time to change the subject. (More on capturing and maintaining the audience's attention later.) When there's a total lack of eye contact, you can even go so far as to say, "I won't take up much more of your time" or "I'll let you go in a second . . ." or just ask a question right back, which allows the other person to talk and give his or her own answer (because nobody thinks their own answer is boring!). This technique re-focuses the person so that when it's your time to speak again, he or she will be paying better attention.

The Twinge

As someone who asks a lot of questions for her job—and many of them difficult ones—I'm always attune to any signs of discomfort or displeasure. The split-second frown or cocking of the head to one side are among the signs that what you're saying isn't sitting well with the other person.

Sometimes the reaction is pretty obvious, like when I asked the attorney for a tech company why the company didn't remove bullying comments from its website. At first her eye started pulsating. As she continued avoiding my questions, she started briskly walking away. Chances are, you're never going to escalate an interaction to what I did next: chasing the woman down the street, thrusting a microphone in her face, using brut verbal strength to get her to 'fess up to her company's wrongdoings. This was not real everyday life. But since your goal is to have a civilized, successful conversation where the other person comes away having heard what you said and feeling positive, as soon as that first twitch, neck rubbing, or forced smile appears, know it's time to change the subject, go into damage control, and use kid gloves.

THE ART OF BEING BLUNT (EAST COASTING)

Here in California, I can spot them from a mile away. East Coasters. Particularly people from New York City and Boston. And having grown up in Connecticut, I consider myself to be one. East Coasters have mastered the art of reaction. Maybe not in the way where road rage–charged drivers will step out of their cars to fistfight in the street (yes, I have seen this on several occasions) or how I once witnessed a man thwack a taxi with his briefcase when the cab failed to yield for a pedestrian. There is something useful to be gleaned from the in-your-face fearlessness and the fast pace of folks from the major cities in the Northeast.

In every newsroom I've worked in, people know I'm coming around the corner based on my footstep frequency, which hits the pavement at a 1.5- to 3-times speed compared to everyone else. Decades ago psychologists Marc and Helen Bornstein proved there is a correlation between walking speed and the pace of life in a city. This escalated pace is my signal to the world that I'm busy and on a mission and can't take time to stop and chat about your weekend/dog's neutering/why astronauts grow six inches while living in space at zero-gravity.

This being said, when I get caught in someone's verbal vortex (when someone just can't stop talking and the whirlwind of words traps me in their cyclone) I usually excuse myself and walk away with conviction, as if I have something important to do. The other person usually understands. However, sometimes despite the social cue as loud as a foghorn there will be people who just don't get it.

This brings me to a well-intentioned colleague we'll call Gerald. You probably have your own Gerald. You know, the co-worker who, when you see him walking toward your desk, your first inclination is to get up and speed walk to the restroom to avoid engaging in any kind of conversation. Or rather, to avoid being the victim of his word waterfall, which usually has to do with his childhood growing up in Tanzania, or what he made himself for dinner the night before.

So it began with my Gerald. The exchanging of pleasantries and asking how my weekend was. Without listening to my response, Gerald dove deep into his day's one-way conversation. This time it was about eco-friendly gardening and the importance of composting. (The man clearly possesses a wide range of interests.) Intentionally turning my shoulders away from him, making uninterested-sounding murmurings, and not engaging about my own composting habits didn't seem to faze him. He just kept going. Gerald was at the point of telling me about the difference between conventionally produced fertilizers and independently sourced manure when I got desperate and decided to get up and briskly walk toward the restroom. He would surely get the idea and leave me alone. But to my horror, as I excused myself rather abruptly, he *followed me* around the corner, down the hall, and kept talking even as I opened the restroom door. He kept talking after I went inside and waited for me after I was finished! It was unreal. Then and there I decided I could stay subtle no longer. Something had to be done or I would never finish my assignment now . . . or ever. I had to channel my East Coast personality.

As he followed me back to my desk for round two of unilateral random talks, I turned around and physically stopped him in his tracks. Firmly but with a kind tone, I said to Gerald, "Hey, can we pick up this conversation again later? I've got so much to do today and I'm running behind!"

To my surprise, Gerald nodded and without missing a beat said, "Oh yeah, sure. I've got so much to do, too. Thanks for the chat! We'll catch up again soon!" Amazing. The three-minute beeline to the ladies room may have set me back three minutes, but it also prompted me to realize how sometimes it's best to just be direct with even the most well-intentioned colleagues. That trip to the restroom helped me realize not everyone can pick up on social cues like I could. Instead of being overly sensitive in not hurting someone's feelings, a well-phrased, polite but blunt message can solve this and many other office challenges.

REACTION REGRET
(THE ICE BUCKET CHALLENGE)

So, what happens if your reaction wasn't the right one? If only there was a magical wand that allows you to erase a phrase as it comes out of your mouth. Or a feature where emails and text messages could magically retract and un-send themselves. Or spontaneously combust, "Mission Impossible"–style, before the intended recipient actually receives and reads it.

While I may not have ever sent drunken text messages to an ex (or at least not that I remember), the gut response and knee-jerk reactions to fire off an email can have serious consequences. I learned this the hard way in the summer of 2014.

This was the time when the idea of pouring frigid ice water over someone's head to raise money for ALS, also known as Lou Gehrig's disease, morphed into a dare that swept the country and the world. These short, oftentimes hilarious videos went viral, raising $115 million and the ALS Ice Bucket Challenge officially became the trendy thing to do.

TV news talent were not immune. (If you Google "Ice Bucket Challenge TV news anchors," you will find videos of hundreds of on-air talent having water poured over their coiffed hairdos and pressed suit jackets.) So when I offered in the afternoon meeting to do a story on the movement and then participate with my coanchor, before I could even utter the word "challenge," I was shocked to be abruptly cut off.

"Uh-uh. We are not doing something everyone has already done before. It's old news. We're moving on," barked a manager.

I was furious. Not only had the manager not allowed me to finish my sentence, she humiliated me by shooting me down in front of my whole team. On top of it, I knew deep down I was right. The story wasn't old. There were many ways to make it fresh with local angles and new study results. My colleagues even approached me after the meeting and said they were on my side.

Without thinking, feeling invincible after the reinforcement from my counterparts, I fired off an email to the entire newsroom which said, in part: "**Reasons why the ice bucket challenge matters.**" The email was written almost entirely in bold, capital letters . . . and in a 72-point font size. It listed not only different angles to the story we could cover, but included links to stories by other stations across the country. It was more background research than was needed for a documentary, let alone for a 90-second TV news story. In hindsight, this was absurd on many levels, but at the time, in the heat of the moment, all I wanted to do was lash out in a passive aggressive email.

I hit "send."

This, I shamefully admit, was a very, very bad move. My boss called me into the office that day and said I was out of line and showed poor leadership. What I really wanted to do was scream back at the top of my lungs, "But I'm *right*! Everybody thought I was right!" But instead, I just looked stone-faced at her, trying to cover up my defensiveness for lashing out via email. It took several months to win back her trust and the trust of my news team. Had I taken a couple of hours to process the events of the morning and instead sent a private email to my manager making my case for why the story was timely and valuable, I could have avoided this entire uncomfortable mess. So, what are some of the strategies you can do if you face a similar situation?

Force Yourself to Step Back

This is often the hardest thing to do in the heat of the moment. As I mentioned earlier in this chapter, I got into the habit of writing the email I'd *like* to send (it's important you do not include the recipient's email address just in case you accidentally hit "send") and then immediately minimizing the window. Not visually seeing the email and then forgetting about it for an hour or two did wonders because once I would revisit the draft, I'd realize how badly it was written, or how my point of view had softened. More times than not, I'd realize an email wasn't necessary at all, or it would need to be overhauled and sent with a clear head.

Responding IRL (Text Slang for "In Real Life"):
Face It Head-On

If the Ice Bucket Challenge incident was an example of how to take pause and think things through before reacting via email, what about in real life? There is no "draft" button to partially say what you want to get off your chest. There is no hiding behind a computer screen to avoid someone in the office. You sometimes need to face things head-on, and immediately.

Remy was in charge of entering reporter graphics into stories before each newscast. A 1970s music enthusiast who had been to practically every Grateful Dead concert in the band's history, she was known for wearing giant Beats by Dre headphones while working. This was such a strange dichotomy; we all would stop by her desk and joke that she was listening to Eminem or Lil' Kim instead of groovy California-hippie rock. Remy was easygoing except for the golden hour before each newscast. The incense-sniffing flower child would morph into a high-strung, perpetually stressed woman of Wall Street.

One day, when I was racing against the clock to get my story out of editing and into the server for airtime, I asked Remy if she could assist in entering the name graphic of a disgraced gymnastics coach into my story. I knew she wouldn't be happy, but I didn't feel I had any choice. I still had so many other things to do, like write a web script and Tweet! My fears were affirmed, and she yelled back, "Why don't you learn how to do it yourself? I'm so busy right now!"

Woah.

Dumbfounded by Remy's unexpected, out-of-character outburst, I stopped what I was doing, maniacally banged on my keyboard to enter in my own name graphic and subtitle. Graphics is not my strong suit and it took me at least three times as long as it would have for Remy. Sure, we reporters were encouraged to do things like this ourselves, but we work as a team and our number one priority job was to file the story. There were always producers and assistants around who were supposed to be ready in a pinch to help us to the finish line.

With the clock tick, tick, ticking, I hit "save" and realized I had just gotten the name in by a hair-splitting, nail-biting, breathless 17 seconds. My Asian DNA and lack of enzymes to process alcohol usually means I don't drink often but after that stomach acid–inducing experience, I needed a double on the rocks. Of anything.

Once my heart stopped pounding, I sat back and thought about how to proceed. There were a few ways to deal with this. Part of me wondered if I should just sweep this incident under the rug and forget about it. Surely Remy and I would go back to joking about rappers and thug music tomorrow. But I knew this problem needed to be taken care of right away. If you have these situations at your office, you need to deal with them as well—and here's why:

Is there a chance the scenario will happen again?

In my case, Remy and I overlapped shifts three days a week and I couldn't avoid her forever. There would undoubtedly be another time where I'd have to ask her for graphics again. Maybe if I knew she was a one-time client or patient I would never treat again, I would let it go . . . but I passed by Remy's tie-dyed workspace almost daily.

It affects your workflow and psyche going forward.

It does not create a positive workplace to have the uncomfortable feeling of unresolved issues with someone who is crucial to your workflow. Incidents like this get ingrained in your mind and make for awkward elephant-in-the-room vibes.

Like the emails strategy of waiting a short period before responding, I finished out the newscasts for the night and strode over to Remy's patchouli-scented desk. She was eating her dinner and looked up when I casually said, "Hey, are we cool?" Turns out her busy deadline-in-mind mindset caused her not to even realize how abrasive she had been toward me. She even thanked me for taking the time to talk to her to see if everything was alright and we've been cool ever since.

No Offense, But Yeah, I'm Offended

Why do some people feel the need to say "no offense" before proceeding with insulting you? Is that phrase somehow supposed to soften the blow of a dis? Those two words, according to Merriam-Webster dictionary, are words "used before a statement to say that one does not want the person or group that one is speaking to feel hurt, angry or upset by what one is about to say." But typically what follows does make people feel "hurt, angry and upset." Shouldn't we all be civilized enough to choose words what wouldn't offend in the first place so there is no need for this kind of phrase? Because honestly, those two words do not preemptively excuse you from directly insulting another person.

A photographer once told me, "No offense, but you're kind of a pushover. I mean, if you had more experience you'd know this story was not a good one and you would have said something to the managers." While I wasn't offended, his comment simply wasn't true. Little did he know, an entire morning meeting full of managers from different departments thought the story (something to do with heavy traffic due to a day of festivals and an impending mega tech conference) was a must-run for the day. Oh, and the experience part? The guy had a mere three more years expertise than I and one of those years didn't count because he was working in the sports department, not news.

Suddenly, the light bulb went off in my head. This dude wasn't even trying to hide his disparaging remarks. He was taking out his disdain for the story on me. These kinds of people don't justify an answer but can be put in their place rather easily with the proper neutral approach.

Completely deadpan I said, "News judgment varies a lot. I know photographers don't usually get to be in the morning meeting like managers and have their say."

My reaction was purposefully neutral because I didn't want to make him feel defensive and have the urge to insult me again. Plus, if he answered the question (which I'm sure he did, silently in his mind at least) he would see that he had no excuse to complain about the assignment or accuse me of poor story selection since he didn't proffer up a better story or offer feedback to the team on what he deemed worthy of covering.

You can bet that was the last time he ever called me a pushover to my face. Remember: If someone is being disrespectful and completely off base, you don't always have to answer head-on. Responding with a comment (not a question) that doesn't address the disparaging remark at all, yet gets them to question what they just said can be a most effective tool in sending a message that you cannot and will not allow this to happen again.

POWER OF BEING STILL
(STAY SILENT TO GET THE LOUDEST RESULTS)

Sometimes the most powerful reaction is none at all. I know. This sounds counterintuitive. Why would I write a book on communication and preach the efficacy of doing nothing? Because communicating efficiently is equal parts words, actions, and making choices. And sometimes, that choice is realizing that being still makes the loudest impression.

The Knee-Jerks and Yellers
(Not the Name of an Indie Band)

Little did I know when I picked up the phone to take my executive producer's (EP for short) phone call my eardrum would be on the verge of bursting.

"I TOLD YOU THE STORY NEEDED TO BE IN 20 MINUTES BEFORE THE NEWSCAST! WHAT DIDN'T YOU UNDERSTAND ABOUT THAT? UNNNGGGGHHHH. GOODBYE!"

Frantically, with the phone still pressed to my ear, I glanced up at the clock in the live van and panicked. It was 18 and a half minutes before the 11 p.m. newscast. My story was being fed into transmission a whole 90 seconds past my EP's requested time. To top it all off, this was still my first week on the job.

I had never in my life had to submit a story a whopping 20 minutes before showtime (usually anywhere between 5 and 10 minutes early was considered the norm) and I was willing to bet no other station in the country required this either. Since I was the new kid, still learning the new computer systems and feeling out different personalities, I didn't know how to react to her harsh tone.

Yelling is something I can't stand (and almost never do) because it never accomplishes anything. Instead of productivity and motivation and teamwork, it creates fear, animosity, and an unhappy work environment. A former news director once mandated the on-air team "not be afraid to yell to get your point across" to writers and producers who made typos or errors in our scripts. After trying it once and nearly making my usually gruff, rugged, grown male producer in a tattered Ozzy Osbourne sweatshirt cry, I didn't have the heart to do it again. Turns out, talking to someone directly and in the right tone (not at a decibel level akin to a jackhammer) is much more effective and empowering.

And having this person yell at me was not something I was willing to put up with. At this point in my career I wasn't afraid to stand up for myself or put my foot down to say, "Yelling at me is wrong and disrespectful. Do not do it again." So I was ready to give her a piece of the business.

As I picked up the phone and relayed to Jordan, my photographer, what I was about to do he thrust out his hand and blocked the phone's dial pad. He said, "Stop. You don't even have to tell me. Teena does this to everyone." Jordan continued, "This isn't how to do it. She doesn't respond to confrontation."

So what did she respond to? According to Jordan, nothing. It would take me about six months to earn her trust through consistent hard work. I'd have to show her I was good at my job and could submit stories absurdly early and only then could I submit my stories 10 minutes before deadline without feeling Teena's wrath.

Turns out Jordan was right. By month three Teena's megaphone mouth had tempered and by month six we were chatting about our love of late-night takeout Thai food and how we've seen every episode of "The Golden Girls." Never again was I required to submit my story 20 minutes before deadline.

Ultimately, do I think her yelling is a problem, wrong, and something that it doesn't belong in a workplace? Absolutely. But if she had lasted at the station for 25 years and won the team a multitude of awards and recognition, I suppose it was something that could be dealt with—for six months at least.

Still Be Still

It can be one of the hardest things to do to not respond to someone who has challenged you. Not doing anything to defend myself during my break-in period with Teena nearly drove me to pulling out my hair in frustration some nights. It feels like being on a low-carb/paleo/trendy diet and walking past one of those mall cinnamon bun shops where the scent of sticky sweet pastries made from refined white flour wafts through the air and acts like a pastry magnet. It takes every ounce of brute strength and willpower not to respond or react and to eat the banana instead. In the end, you feel proud of yourself and even more accomplished when you don't feel bloated the next day.

But first, before you can ever put being still into practice, know when to use this technique. Not everyone is open to talking things through and solving problems. Nor are they deserving of your energy and time.

Use Calculated Silence When It's Deserved

"He what!?" I exclaimed into the phone as a line of crabby people in need of their morning caffeine fix listened. I didn't even care that they all turned their heads to see what crazy lady just had a mini-outburst in the middle of the Blue Bottle coffee shop. Without caring what everyone thought (or who recognized me from TV) I kept muttering over and over to myself: "I should have listened to my gut. I should have listened to my gut." That phrase

played on a continuous loop for weeks in my head after I got off the phone with a friend of mine who owned a large marketing company in San Francisco.

"Yeah, Dion. It was so weird. In my 38 years doing this, I've never encountered anyone who would do that. It definitely wasn't a mistake," said my friend.

Let's rewind.

Just two weeks earlier, my friend took a meeting with a man named Vince, who I had met after he reached out to me on Instagram wanting to connect. Looking back, that was red flag number one. Usually, I found random men who reached out to me via social media wanting to have coffee/tea/lunch pretty alarming as they usually had ill intentions. After weeks of messaging, a coworker told me he was harmless and I should message him back and meet up for a meal. I had only worked with this colleague four, maybe five, times. That was red flag number two. After doing a little investigative journalism on Vince's Instagram profile and saw he had a decent following for his sunset/landscape photography, I responded to his message and agreed to have avocado toast with him on my day off. Because he had so many fans, he must be an okay individual, right? Looking back, I had a sea of red flags just waving in my face, yet I didn't see any of them before it was too late.

The lunch ended up going well and after he expressed wanting to meet more people and build his business connections for his photography, I offered to help introduce him to some of my cohorts. In return I asked him to take photographs at the community events I attended so I could use them for my social media, my website, and this very book. Over the course of several months we met regularly over coffee or food to plan out ways to collaborate. He took photos as I went on location for a *Crazy Rich Asians* screening and interviewed a former Olympian who was cohosting. He got to meet the athlete and the team and I had killer photos to document the evening. I invited him to all the events I participated in and for a while this seemed like a win-win.

But when he asked me to help a friend at a competing station build her brand in tandem with the nonprofit work I was doing, I flat out said, "No." This woman didn't have the best reputation and she was known for showing up late to events. This wasn't the type of brand I wanted to associate with—plus, she was employed by my competition.

Vince's response was to completely melt down via text. He accused me of being selfish, wouldn't return my calls to hash out the situation, and said I was never his friend. My attempts to reach out so he could clarify what he meant and talk through his raging emotions were shut down with a "have a nice life" and passive-aggressive smile emoji. To make matters worse, he bailed on all of our open projects.

My marketing friend had set him up with an exclusive private tour of a San Francisco landmark building so he could take photos from 1,000 feet up in the air. Vince not only stood up the executive of the company, but my friend had to cover for his bad behavior. He also retracted his offer to help shoot a nonprofit's inaugural gala. This one was particularly infuriating as he was letting down hundreds upon hundreds of young people with disabilities. Now that's just selfish and cold.

My husband, Evan, seeing how hurt I was from Vince's betrayal had to remind me almost daily for more than a week that I did nothing wrong. Evan helped me realize Vince didn't deserve my friendship, help, or that of my network. After dedicating so much time and effort, and a wealth of resources to someone only to have him cut you off, refuse to engage in problem-solving, and then screw over your trusted friends, is very disheartening.

It is completely okay not to forgive and equally as okay not to forget. I don't care how many books have been written on the subject or what Oprah has told us. It's been drilled into my head to try to make amends whenever possible, but sometimes other people's behavior is simply inexcusable! What if I had forgiven and forgotten about Vince's unprofessionalism and it happened again, but to a much worse degree? It was simply not worth the risk and I never attempted to text or call him again. Months later, when he tried to rekindle our friendship by reaching out (and not apologizing), it was my turn not to respond, and I deleted his number for good.

This decision to stop engaging with someone who had caused so many issues ended up being a blessing. The beauty of communicating by *not* communicating is that the ball is in your court, and you hold the ability to focus on moving forward and kicking butt instead of wasting precious time and mental fortitude on how you're going to navigate around someone else's bad behavior! In lieu of dedicating more time to fixing a relationship with someone not deserving of it, imagine the possibilities of where your energy can go instead! In my case, the nonprofit ended up scoring not one but two great drama-free photographers to capture me on stage, after I raised nearly $50,000 for the cause without Vince's help. Another nice side effect of choosing to cut off communication with those who don't respect you or your craft? Motivation to succeed and the self-realization that you hold the power to thrive.

The Interpersonal Battlefield
Navigating the Awkward,
the Unexpected,
the Downright Bizarre

CHILDHOOD TRAINING GROUND

Y KNACK FOR understanding the fine nuances of communication came not only from being on the job, but much earlier, growing up in America's breadbasket. Small towns in Michigan, Ohio, and later Connecticut, where I was often one of just a handful of Asian kids, meant I was hyperaware of every stare from WGs (white girls) because of my dorky self-administered bowl-cut hairstyle and Goodwill overalls. If that weren't enough, try bringing shredded pork floss and milky white steam buns to school instead of the super-cool Lunchables and Capri Sun and see what happens.

It became very apparent to me in elementary school that the world was not ready for me and my family. Memories of how I stuck out among my peers overshadowed the happy memories of birthday parties and going to my friend Carolyn's house to play with her Playmobil dollhouse. Instead, much of what I remember includes the man at the supermarket who suspiciously eyed my mother as if to accuse her of stealing when she got too close to the high-ticket saffron in the spice aisle. (In reality, she was just getting close to examine the bottle because the deviled ham from a can and Country Crock sandwiches on Wonder bread she made for my breakfast never required this kind of flavoring and seemed totally foreign.)

Little did I know navigating all these situations would be a training ground for me to grow adept at identifying people who were masters at communication. These were people who didn't shift eye contact when I was talking. (What? There were people who were interested in what I had to say?) These were the adults who let out genuine guttural laughs at my lame knock-knock jokes instead of the forced, fake "hehs." Then there were the generous, kindhearted people who became my mentors and close friends who made me feel like I was the only person in the room and gave me their full attention whenever I opened my mouth.

As an employee in your organization, you are probably aware that these subtle reactions happen every hour of the day. By learning to read people's subtle and overt reactions, including body language and facial expressions, and applying some of the techniques I'll share in this chapter, you too can become a master of navigating common communication situations.

THE SOCIAL BERMUDA TRIANGLE: BEING LEFT OUT OF CONVERSATIONS

This common workplace phenomenon happens when three people are chatting, and two people decide to talk about something completely foreign to the third person. Most of the time it doesn't happen on purpose but when it does, it leaves the third person feeling left out or sometimes wanting to leave the conversation.

My most dreaded moments have always been the "cross-talk" between the two anchors and sports person at the end of the sports segment. For one thing: I know very little about sports and don't have a particular interest in men who tackle each other to the turf, nor do I care what R-B-I stands for. Feigning an interest, one night during the 11 p.m. newscast in Charlotte, I blurted out "Goooooo baseball!" The reaction from my on-air counterparts was crickets, followed by uncontrollable laughter as soon as we hit the commercial break. I had just made the lamest contribution to a sports conversation ever.

The most successful conversations are the ones where every person is able to contribute to the topic. It's the "inside baseball" stories, jokes, or references that alienate and make others feel like they're not in the loop. Nobody likes to feel uneducated or like an outsider. Even the most skilled conversationalists can struggle in a dialogue with someone who is babbling about vintage Pez dispensers from the 1960s. Having a debate about why "Saved by the Bell" is superior to "Beverly Hills 90210" is difficult with someone who hasn't seen either television show.

If you really can't tear yourself away from the idea of sharing an obscure factoid or inserting a bit of commentary into a conversation, go ahead and get it off your chest. But before everyone else in the party leaves, steer the ship back to where the conversation needs to be: with everyone contributing. As a professional poker player, my husband often talks about royal flushes, full houses, or being on-tilt with a group of card enthusiasts. But if one person doesn't even know how to play the game, I'll chime in, "Hey, I don't play either. I once lost $7 and started crying!" to get that one person to feel included. If you find yourself in a similar situation, put yourself in that person's shoes, and think about what would make you more comfortable in that moment.

FIND COMMON GROUND:
HOW TO MASTER THE SIDE CHAT

Here's something you learn about humans: After interviewing thousands of people in my career, I've realized one thing. No matter where we live and no matter our socioeconomic background, we all generally share the same emotions and human responses. Love, happiness, and hurt. This is common ground. It's why small talk often consists of talking about the weather, where someone is from, and where their families are. We all experience these things in some form or another, making it an easy conventional topic everyone can weigh in on. There are plenty of methods in which we get to a mutual understanding and everyone is included. If you are at a workplace function or even in an informal meeting and need to break the ice, the following are some strategies I have found extremely effective.

Find the Lowest Common Denominator

This is as easy as boiling down a topic to the very core. Faced with a conversation at work or at a mixer involving a brainy scientist who spent the past 10 years in South Africa researching fauna and flora? The lowest common denominator: What is the most general thing this confusing topic is about? Plants and travel. You may have no idea about scientific gibberish, but you can easily ask a question or make a comment about how certain plants give you allergies or how your sister used to plant rare roses in the backyard. You've never been to South Africa, but you hear there are penguins that inhabit the western coast. By identifying what is most common to nonspecialists of the topic is the first step to steering the conversation back to an effective and enjoyable place.

Find a roundabout way to then interject something about your own self into the conversation. For example, I have colleagues who enjoy talking about fighter jets, Boeing 727s, and the Hawker 800 private jets. While they're laughing and enjoying themselves, others around them tend to feel alienated, including me. The extent of my own aviation knowledge is knowing who Amelia Earhart was. But I have been to an airshow. It was breathtaking and jaw-droppingly inspiring to see men and women take on challenges like 360 spins and turns and all those loop-de-loop flight moves I have no clue the names of. Maybe this, then, turns into a conversation about what the correct terms are. Or, if they have ever been to an airshow themselves. By finding the most general part of even the most specialized topic, inserting what little you do know about the subject and then coupling it with a question keeps the other person engaged and feeling heard while giving you something to talk about and feeling included.

JUST KIDDING! NOT!

One of the most common workplace challenges is getting across information or an unpopular point of view in an inoffensive way.

One of my favorite ways of addressing a serious topic is to soften the question, statement, or suggestion with a joke. Laugher is an equalizer: you can be the head of a multi-billion-dollar corporation, a migrant worker, or a fashion designer. No matter who you are, laughter and maybe a dash of absurdity takes a potentially serious topic and makes it comfortable enough to discuss.

I learned this strategy at a young age.

For most of my childhood, I thought my family was poor. Special occasions to McDonald's to get a cheeseburger Happy Meal meant going through the drive-through (we almost never went inside the restaurant itself) where Mom would open the door to our beat-up air-condition-less Mazda minivan, peer outside, and reach down to collect whatever loose change was on the ground. If the bounty of random coins was good, I'd slink down in my seat and hide with embarrassment as she'd use the change to pay for the $1.99 meal. Later (sometimes on the same day) at the Goodwill, she'd butter up the cashier, complimenting her on her nails or hair and then ask if she could have the senior citizen discount for those over age 60. Since she was probably only in her early forties at the time, this seemed like a bold-faced lie. When the teenager ringing her up nodded in agreement, my mom would roll with the punches and accept the 20 percent off. If not, she'd say, "Just joking!" followed by an incredulous exclamation, "Do I look 60!?" and proceed to pay full price for our Cornflower CorningWare casserole set. Oftentimes the cashier was so taken aback by this seemingly meek, mild Asian lady paying for her merchandise with change in a clear baggie that they'd give her the discount anyway!

Turns out, I learned later on as an adult, we weren't poor. My mom was just freakin' frugal. This thriftiness didn't exactly rub off on me, but the humor part did. Subconsciously, I comprehended the power of something that is seemingly a joke and how it could be a good way to communicate what you want by testing the waters.

While I know you're not bargaining for cookware at work, using this half-joking-but-not-really tactic is a great way to get your point across or ask for something when you're not fully comfortable. Case in point: My boss asked me to come in on my day off (despite being almost three hours away on a mini road trip) to anchor for a woman who called out sick. He came over to my desk later in the day to thank me for sacrificing my leisure time with friends. As much as I appreciated the station's belief in me to fill some pretty big shoes (at the time I was anchoring a less high-profile show) and the extra exposure to the audience, it was getting a little old since this had been the third time in six weeks I was called in on my day off. I believed it was important to make sure my boss knew how my willingness to work meant I was a valuable team player and worth keeping around. So, I added semi-jokingly, "Just remember that when we renegotiate my contract!" The manager smiled knowingly and said, "Oh yes, trust me, I will remember." So, without having to directly ask, I got answers to (1) whether my enthusiasm to help out the team was appreciated and (2) if the station wanted to re-sign me at the end of my term.

GLOSS AND GO: THE BRILLIANT BRUSH-OFF

Sometimes you need a more serious strategy than laughing something off. I know this well. I had just committed the cardinal sin of coanchors: the stealing of the sign-off. In the TV news biz, anchors use a tagline at the end of the newscast such as, "Have a good evening" or "May your day ahead be better than the one before" to signal the end of the show and act as a gesture of gratitude or a final farewell to the audience. Edward R. Murrow, the godfather of journalism, used the sign-off "Good night and good luck." Hugh Downs, the former anchor of "20/20" (who, along with Barbara Walters, unknowingly helped me learn English—no "The Magic Schoolbus" show in the Lim household), used the line "We're in touch so you be in touch." In the Will Ferrell movie *Anchorman*, Ron Burgundy's was "Stay Classy San Diego."

During my morning years, mine was "Have a quality day, friends." Later, when I was in Tampa my coanchor Reggie's tagline of "Have a good night and do take care" was so well-known after nearly 30 years in the market, viewers would shout it out in the streets when he was nearby or when they would see me at the grocery store and ask me to tell him, "Do take care."

A number of years before he and I began working together, Reggie's desk partner—we'll call her Marcia—let a "Do take care" slip at the end of the show. Reggie laughed like a Buddha recalling the story and jokingly said viewers were going to call in to complain she stole his line . . . which they did. In droves! But at the end of the day, Reggie took it all in stride. It was funny and made for an entertaining story of how personally connected the audience felt to those eight words.

Phil, another anchor I worked with later on, was not so forgiving. At all.

For some reason I had gotten confused listening to my director's countdown in my earpiece and didn't hear my coanchor say, "Have an enjoyable evening and see you tomorrow" so I subconsciously let a "Have an enjoyable evening" slip out.

Before I could even close out my scripts on the iPad and shut down the computer, Phil barked, "That's my line. Mine. I tell people to have an enjoyable evening. Nobody else. I've been saying it for almost as many years as you've been alive."

I was shocked. Was a grown man really that upset I wanted our viewers to have an enjoyable evening? It then got worse.

"I already said it. Why would you say it again?" grumbled Phil.

Granted, it wasn't smooth of me to repeat what he said, but I hadn't heard him say it because I was distracted trying to listen to the director who was counting me down in my ear. Why was he getting mad about something I did anyway? If anyone looked awkward it was me, not him.

Phil, in his expensive suit, monogrammed cuff links, and silk Hermes pocket square was having a man-baby tantrum.

How do you handle yourself after someone knowingly humiliates you in front of your peers? Over something so seemingly trivial and silly? He was essentially sending a beacon to everyone listening (not only a meteorologist and a sports anchor, but also the entire behind-the-scenes crew in the control room who heard the exchange over headsets) indicating I didn't maneuver the final minutes of the show as deftly as he could. I was inferior and rude for taking his line.

There were many ways to handle this bizarre circumstance and I knew this one had to be managed with a certain expertise, as Phil was known for not backing down on his convictions. In his ego-inflated head he was always right. I wasn't scared to put him in his place, because I was used to confronting shady PR professionals and tight-lipped attorneys who didn't want to answer my probing questions. But unlike these people, whom I would use all my verbal brute strength on and never run into again, I had to work with Phil in close proximity on a daily basis.

This was a time to exercise the Gloss and Go. Let me explain.

First: Do Not Apologize

Sometimes it's not necessary to apologize, even if you're guilty of something. For those who knee-jerk react with anger at something so trivial, they do not deserve an expression or gesture of regret. Was I sorry I took his line? Sure. But not sorry he tried to humiliate me in front of my team. When you are at work, you and your colleagues are equals. And there should be a certain level of respect. By apologizing I would show weakness, and he would think he had the upper hand. For adult-babies, an apology is affirmation that they're right and what they've done is acceptable. Someone needs to send the message that their actions are not okay and offering up an "I'm sorry" is not the way to do it.

Second: When They're Enraged, Do Not Engage

When people are so enraged for seemingly trivial things, all logic and reason go out the window. In their clouded furor no degree of reasoning will be accepted. I knew Phil could not be reasoned with, so I chose not to engage and explain what had happened. The logic would be lost in his cloud of anger.

Third: Deflect and Gloss

Deflecting shouldn't be as obvious as pointing over the person's shoulder, and yelling, "Look! It's a bird! It's a plane!" It also works best when the topic is closely related. After Phil had a moment to catch his breath from the first wave of tongue-lashing, I immediately went into the story about Marcia and how viewers called in spades accusing Marcia of being a sentence-stealer but how Reggie thought it was funny. The hope was to tell Phil a similar story of this happening to someone else, so he would be too preoccupied listening or processing the story to notice I did not apologize.

Ultimately the strategy worked and later in the evening, Phil seemed to have forgotten about his stolen sign-off and we went back to work as usual.

KISSING ONE'S BUTT (IS IT EVER OKAY?)

If you find yourself in a situation where someone's ego threatens to run the show, a little stroking of that ego can often work to your advantage and get you where you want to be.

Before I started working with an established colleague who had written a book on storytelling and the art of journalism, my new teammates pulled me aside and said if I told him I owned his book and used it in college (which was true) he would be nicer to me. This seemed ludicrous but I followed through on their recommendation and it worked. On occasion, he would smile in my direction instead of staring with his usual furrowed brow, deep-in-thought, scowling expression.

Just like consuming butter and sweets, I strongly suggest using pandering sparingly. A producer friend of mine, Cammie, once told me a story about working with a diva anchor on a promotional spot featuring her new health segment. Since Diva Anchor had been in the market a long time (more than 23 years, as she liked to remind everyone she encountered, probably even the cashier at the Dunkin' Donuts drive-thru), she had an ego the size of Texas. They were at a local park where Cammie shot video of the anchor jumping rope and doing other various activities that promote heart health. The anchor was upset that her hair kept bouncing around while doing the exercises (um, that usually is what happens, unless your hair is shellacked so hard with hair spray that it becomes a helmet) she made Cammie waste an additional two hours waiting for the wind to die down, shooting and rerecording the lines until her hair looked perfectly arranged.

Cammie said she was exasperated and her pleas to hasten the shoot fell on deaf ears. Then a harebrained Hail Mary idea struck her like lightning. She turned to her anchor, who was dabbing her nose with a powder puff, and said, "Listen. You're such a big deal in the city, everyone knows your name and loves you. They'll love you even more if you can show them you sweat and get your hair messy just like the commoners!"

Commoners? What?! Had we just tele-transported back to Ancient Rome and our viewers were plebeians? Playing into the anchor's own ego was just what she needed to get moving and wrap up the shoot. Cammie's strategy to kiss up just enough worked.

When satisfying someone's ego, just don't lose sight of how ridiculous the situation. Remember, the end goal is to work with the person toward a common goal. If this is what it takes, so be it. Just don't lose sight of why you're doing it and don't make it a habit.

WHEN BLUNTNESS BOMBS

In Chapter 1, I talked about how a blunt response can save you from being cornered by the office chatterbox. The workplace isn't the only place that could benefit from some bluntness. How about the entire planet? Instead of guessing how your crush feels about you, wouldn't it be nice if he or she just came right out and said it? No more beating around the bush when you don't like the way your fellow nurse applies tourniquets to patients. In TV news, time is at a premium and communications must be conveyed quickly and efficiently. Being direct and to the point is sometimes the only way to get things done.

When time is of the essence and your message needs to get across in an attention-grabbing way, if you execute the bluntness correctly it's a supremely effective way to communicate. But not everybody can handle the truth. Sometimes the resulting reaction may not be comfortable, but it can not only solve the problem at hand but tell a lot about your working relationship with that person.

My ability to be direct (and sometimes misunderstood as being insensitive) comes from a strict Tiger Mom (yes, it's not just the catchy name of a book—it's a real Asian mother phenomenon) whose pointedness often reduced me to tears as a child. Imagine a key-lime plaid, button-down shirt presented to her on her fifty-first birthday that yielded an, "Aye-ya! Mama don't wear this! Give to Salvation Army!" (It's not that she doesn't care about the gift, it's just her way of saying she prefers to sew and wear her own clothes.) No joke, that was the last time I ever bought her a birthday present.

Blunt (Stink) *Bomb*—When Bluntness Bombs . . . but Also Kind of Works

Behind her back, at least a half-dozen people referred to a former colleague as "Cat Shit Breath." The culprit? A trifecta of nasty habits: chain smoking, drinking what seemed like a gallon of Coke Zero a day, and not brushing her teeth after doing both. With every exhale (and there are a lot of them during the course of a newscast) out wafted the odor of decay.

Since I did care about this person and wanted to prevent her from further ridicule (and save my olfactory senses and nostrils), I had to say something. But how do you do this with tact? Some recommended I put a bottle of Listerine in her cubby. Or sprinkle mints and gum like confetti on her workspace. After some thought, I decided passive-aggressive product placement was not the answer. Others thought I should get a manager to break the news. This wasn't quite right either, as the boss had plenty of much more pressing issues to deal with.

Given how my mom always seemed to get what she wanted (no more terrible birthday presents) by being blunt, I decided to rip off the bandage and tell CSB to her face. But how?

After a particularly stifling mouth odor day on set, I asked CSB to stick around after the stage managers left the studio. Looking her right in the eye, I said, "I need you to brush your teeth." Looking crestfallen she nodded, made up some excuse about her dentist not wanting her to brush her teeth to protect her gums (uh, worst dentist ever), and the problem miraculously was solved by the next day. Sticks of chewing gum appeared on her desk. Within a month she had kicked the smoking habit. I thought things were fine and I had done her a favor. Others in the newsroom noticed and would mention how the stink was gone and no longer called her the horrible nickname. Not once did I tell anyone I was the reason behind the air-clearing.

More than a year later, though, while we disagreed about something I don't even remember, she gave me a fiery look and spat out, "Sometimes people are direct and hurt others' feelings" and let out a deep huff of air in my face, which smelled like cinnamon Dentyne. Whoa, talk about passive-aggressive.

What this experience taught me was that being blunt is an effective tool in achieving what you want. But misjudging the degree of straightforwardness I could use with this person ultimately hurt our relationship. You'll find yourself offending less and achieving more if you can soften the directness by not using such demanding language as, "I need you to XYZ," and say instead, "Hey, there've been some complaints about your breath and it affects me too. Just wanted you to know."

Put Someone Out of Their Misery

Sometimes being direct is a relief for the person you are communicating with. When a reporter colleague of mine casually dropped the fact she knew how to anchor to the general manager, instead of beating around the bush and offering up a "Maybe on holidays" or "Why don't we work on it a bit first" she got a, "You're not ready for the desk, so we'll have to pass on that option."

Instead of pouting or being upset, she said she was relieved! At least a direct answer was better than worrying and wondering, eating up time and mental energy. She now had direction to keep practicing her anchoring and keep kicking butt at reporting.

Remember that when you're answering in a way the other person doesn't expect (or you're receiving an answer you aren't expecting), the result is often valuable information that can potentially help you move forward in your career.

THE NON-APOLOGY APOLOGY

While I strategically chose not to apologize to the anchorman baby, and don't believe in over-apologizing for things you're not really sorry for, an expression of regret does work in some situations.

When a newer reporter I worked with wrote a terrible anchor intro to his story (which was already riddled with typos), I was furious. The three sentences were so packed with errors I could barely understand the meaning of each word. Latin would have been easier to comprehend. Since the script wasn't dropped into the rundown until about two minutes before it aired, I didn't have time to proofread it either. While he was the one who wrote it, guess whose credibility was at stake for hundreds of thousands of people? Mine!

For some reporters I have a rapport with, I would text or in passing casually mention "Yo, what happened to that script? Was that written in English?" But this guy was different. I never saw him in real life since he was always out in the field, and when I did it was only in passing or while meeting at the coffee machine. How should I approach him to get my point across that he needed to be more careful with writing his scripts? I had no idea if he was open to joking and I didn't want a semi-kidding fail.

Instead, I approached his desk and said, "Hey Warren, I'm sorry I butchered your anchor toss the other night . . . the producers were slammed all evening and I should have caught the typos." Warren looked alarmed and said, "Typos? Man, I didn't know there were typos in the piece. That's my fault. I took a call from my mom in the middle of writing that last night. I'll be more careful next time. My bad!" In the same way misery loves company, you can use a genuine apology (yes, in my case I was truly sorry I didn't circumvent the error sooner) to then prompt not only an apology from the other person but what comes with it—acknowledgment of what went wrong and by default, an unspoken message that it won't happen again.

CAN'T WIN WITH THE WHINERS

He. Just. Wouldn't. Stop. Complaining. The story. The weather. The traffic. Terry was my photographer for the day, and clearly he had not just woken up on the wrong side of the bed, he must have stepped in dog poop on the wrong side of the bed. Because on this particular day, there was nothing that could appease Terry into working as a team on the story ahead of us.

We were covering a music festival he had covered many times before but one that I was excited to be at. I was trying to make the story sound, look, and feel different from years past so I asked him to get a couple extra creative shots, which he refused to do. He just shot the story from one stagnant position and then proceeded to waste half an hour shooting the breeze with a photographer from a competing station. Despite trying everything to motivate him ("C'mon, this'll be easy. Let's just get a few people in the crowd with me then we can go.") he just declined, citing it "wasn't necessary" to put any effort into the story.

By constantly vocalizing his indignation I was hindered from doing my job and I would be the one getting in trouble later for not producing a quality product. Instead of collaborating, he shut down every suggestion or idea in favor of grumbling over why he wasn't assigned with someone else, or to a more impactful story. You probably work with people just like this—and know how infuriating it can be to deal with their whining. Next time, try one of the following strategies.

Do Not Succumb

In these situations, the whiner wants you to whine with him. It's the only way he feels better about himself. Terry had baited me with a series of invasive questions, trying to get me to complain about other people. ("Mackenzie is the worst assignment desk editor and never gives me the stories I like . . . don't you agree?") When I didn't partake in throwing my teammates under the bus, he became more irritated. But I refused to sacrifice my own convictions, beliefs, and manners just to satisfy someone's need to gossip and be rude to others behind their backs. It's a great power move to stop whiners in their tracks.

Skirt and Empathize

Instead of allowing yourself to fall deep into the whiner's rabbit hole, the only way to manage one is to skirt around the subject he or she is complaining about and then show empathy. Sometimes this is all a person is looking for. Terry was complaining about how his tripod was heavy. I decided to turn complaining into sympathy: "I can see how lugging around 17 pounds every day with the same arm can be tiring!" Also, adding a personal and relatable story can further help the person identify that you understand. "When I carry your tripod, my arms really hurt, and that's only for a few minutes, not like you, for eight hours." It didn't solve his whining, but it did make it a bit more manageable. He felt like I understood his struggle, putting us on a more even playing field.

The Terry incident proved people who complain are never part of the solution. They never advance and often end up unhappy or fired. So, what do you do when you're faced with an issue? Instead of complaining, solve it so you can showcase what you do best . . . and get a few perks for yourself. The next story is a great example of that.

USE COMMUNICATION DEXTERITY TO SOLVE PROBLEMS AND GET WHAT YOU WANT (NO MATTER WHERE YOU ARE)

While on big vacations, I generally try to stay away from my work phone. As a woman with 2,944 unread emails (many from bad PR professionals who send blast messages about stories I'd never consider covering, like, true story, offering me a free lip plumper to achieve a Kylie Jenner–sized pout) and a dozen unopened text messages, I believe in occasional disconnecting. By checking my phone only once a day while on vacation, I allow my brain to reset, I feel relaxed, and I'm ready to tackle the onslaught of messages when I go back to work.

It was during a sightseeing trip to the Parthenon I glanced down at my inbox while in line for a packet of roasted nuts from a weathered looking street vendor. There, at the top, was a message from my assistant news director asking if I'd like to head to Washington, DC, for the upcoming Brett Kavanaugh hearing two days later. A rough itinerary was included in the body of the message.

My husband looked horrified after I handed him the phone. As a professional poker player, he worked whenever the tables online were juicy. We were used to rearranging plans at the drop of a hat. (This is why we work so well: we understand what we do is important and support it however we can.) But the proposed schedule sounded bonkers. Our vacation itinerary had us set to leave Greece the next day, which was fine. But after a three-hour flight to Germany, nine-and-a-half-hour flight to Chicago, and four-hour flight to San Francisco, it seemed grueling and insane to only spend seven hours on the ground before flying across the country to DC. Not to mention, I'd be cutting my vacation time one day short. Just the thought of it all made me exhausted.

Did I want to do it? Yes and no. It would be much easier to just go home, take my day off and get a manicure, eat a slice of my favorite pizza, and go back to life as usual. But on the other hand, this would be a chance to witness an historic hearing and subsequent vote on a Supreme Court Justice. It would be a chance for me to showcase my abilities to cover hard-hitting political cases (not just the debut of the world's stinkiest flower) and do it for a large audience in almost every newscast on Thursday and Friday. I knew I had to respond to the email ASAP, since this was a hot assignment and one that would be gobbled up by someone else if I declined. But not under the terms proposed.

Complaining doesn't even come to mind anymore when situations like this arise. Not only does it waste time and accomplish nothing (except make you look like a whiner), but after years of working with different managers, I know that no matter their personalities or reactions, complainers never win. Instead, when faced with a conflicting situation, I go into an instant three-step problem-solving mode.

Step One: Figure out what you want.

When friends and colleagues are having a hard time making a decision about something, I ask them, "What do you want?" More times than not I get a furrowed brow and a slight shoulder shrug response. You'd be surprised at how often we get clouded by initial reactions and emotion that we don't clearly spell out why we are reacting the way we do.

In this case, I was caught way off guard. Covering politics was the last thing on my mind and being in the air for so long journeying home seemed outrageous. Who wanted to spend unneeded time in the air, like flying from Greece to San Francisco only to double back and go to DC? It didn't make sense. For cutting my vacation time short, I also wanted an extra day off somewhere. This was a reasonable, logical ask that perhaps the planning team at the station didn't address or think of because of the immediacy of the story.

Step Two: Find solutions before problems.

Preparedness is your preemptive solution to opposition to your proposal. Having the foresight to be armed with an immediate answer before your solution can be challenged shows your conviction for your proposal. It also convinces people that you've spent time thinking out your ideas. In the Kavanaugh case, I took 10 minutes to search flights from Chicago to DC and knew staying a night in a hotel in Chicago and the flight cost would be about the same price as if I were to fly from SFO to Dulles on that crazy seven-hour turnaround flight. My plan would cost the same but would leave me well-rested and more ready to work a crazy 18-hour shift the next day.

Step Three: Remember, it's not about you, it's about them.
When you make your case for your plan, do so succinctly and with conviction, and remember even though it is about you, it's just as much about making life easier and better for the person you are working with. Just as if you're pitching an idea for a new client trying to earn their business, you want to give off the utmost confidence that your idea is not only a smart plan but the only plan to make the end goal a success for the rest of your team.

Less than 30 minutes after proposing the plan to my manager, my administrative assistant had me booked on the flight to Chicago I wanted and at a hotel conveniently located near a place where I could rent a dress for the occasion (my suitcase was filled with shorts and swimsuits, not DC business wear), and as a bonus I could have dinner with a friend who lived in the city. The trip ended up being one of my favorite assignments of my career: chasing down senators on Capitol Hill, meeting passionate changemaking women who had traveled from around the country to make their opinions heard, and doing it all with a photographer who was as enthusiastic and excited to be there as I was. And it worked out for the station, which got a lot of positive feedback from viewers who were impressed to see their local station dedicate the time and energy to the cause. It was a win-win for everyone.

By navigating these problems into a solution using these steps, you'll also benefit beyond solving the issue at hand. It also helps build your reputation as someone who doesn't need to whine, moan, or groan but is self-sufficient and easy to get along with. When you can process and execute what needs to be done to make everyone happy, you demonstrate your willingness to be a team player, and that's an important thing to be able to communicate in any career.

The Betta Fish
Lessons from the
Workplace Fish Tank

S A KID, I was fascinated with betta fish. Also known as Siamese Fighting Fish, these brightly colored aquatic creatures don't swim in schools like other species, but instead prefer to exist alone and choose to fight others to the death in order to reign supreme in the fishbowl. This is why my mom and dad ended up buying me a pair of those orange big-brained, bulging-forehead goldfish instead: they could peacefully (albeit boringly) swim around for years and exist without any issues.

Decades later, as a full-fledged employed adult, I realized the workplace is an aquarium filled with betta fish! But what was worse, these human equivalents didn't use physical violence to show off their neon colors. In some ways, that would be easier to deal with! Instead, these adult human combat creatures used snark, verbal aggression, and underhanded sneaky tactics to take down their prey. And that prey was usually yours truly. What fooled me in the beginning was how it was often the prettiest or the most unlikely workplace counterparts who would end up trying to take you down because you were the new kid in the tank.

You likely know exactly who I'm talking about. Think of Susana in the shipping department who appears to be all smiles and sweetness when she hands you your Amazon Prime packages each week, but on the inside, she's seething because she applied for your job years earlier . . . and didn't get it. For me, my betta fish moment came when a real-life Ron Burgundy from the movie *Anchorman* rigged my teleprompter scripts so I would mess up on-air. Another workplace saboteur leaked embarrassing photos of me to a national news blog. Again, for personal gain. (More on that later.)

The fact I even need to write a chapter about watching your back at all times seems paranoid and preposterous and downright sad. Maybe being in news has exacerbated this need to stay safe and aware of my surroundings. We cover shootings, cases of identity theft, and bank robberies. A bodyguard follows me and my crew if we're shooting in a high-risk area. But none of us have bodyguards in the office where, instead of personal property attacks, we are faced with credibility attacks. These affect your mental state, personal well-being, and ability to do your job.

Humans are inherently competitive beings. Scientists have long claimed that competition is "one of the most basic functions of nature" and that it's an instinct to survive. We "compete for resources in the forms of food, jobs, living quarters and general status in society. We compete against each other, we compete against ourselves and we compete as groups against other groups." Competition at work can motivate . . . or bring out the worst in some.

Hence why this chapter is so needed.

But while you can't have your head on an owl-like swivel at all times, or wear those rearview spy glasses (I also loved those as a kid), or hire a life coach to follow you around at all times, you can learn to peacefully coexist. Swimming around these creatures isn't always enough and, honestly, it's not always possible. (What do you mean I can't trade desks with you?) So, your best ammunition is to fortify yourself with the savvy strategies and quick quips that'll keep you alive and thriving, so you can keep moving upward while those trying to get in the way of your success stay stagnant.

This isn't to say you won't encounter, or be surrounded by phenomenal, supportive, genuine people. Much of who I am today is because of the standout women and men who supported me and held my hand when others couldn't or wouldn't. (More on finding and nurturing these relationships later.) But the fact of the matter is the workplace is a curious amalgam of people from all backgrounds with varying goals. While we should ideally work in tandem for the greater good, it doesn't always happen. Your goal is to rise above it, all the while maintaining a positive working attitude with the people around you. Trust me on this: once you master this part of the workplace and your career, a big chunk of everything else challenging about work will fall into place.

FROM SORORITY/FRATERNITY TO BATTLEFIELD

A fellow reporter friend of mine once told me about the time she waved at and wished a senior female reporter a Happy Thanksgiving only to be dismissed with a haughty "goodbye" and strut out the door. I envisioned it to be like that viral video of rapper Nicki Minaj sashaying down a runway, blonde extensions whipping back and forth, arriving at her exclusive private jet you're not allowed to be on. Except this was a 50-something-year-old woman in a tweed power suit giving a 37-year-old reporter a piece of the business as she stomped away into her news van. My friend, an incredibly intelligent, quick-witted, talented storyteller said she was so shocked she just stood there, mouth agape as the vehicle pulled out of the driveway. The mental image of this was kind of hilarious in a pitiful kind of way.

What happened to civility? What happened to everyone being in the same sorority or living on the same floor of the college dorm, planning out a 1980s movies night? Instead, offices are micro clubs and cliques with a separation between the old guard and any newcomers. On the outside, the existing staff may be the most welcoming, the most cordial people you've ever met. But when you're the new kid in town, there's undoubtedly a hazing period. Your job is to survive it.

LIKE MURDER:
THERE'S ALWAYS A MOTIVE

In a way there is reason to think a bit like a true crime episode on the Oxygen network when you're at work. Is your colleague taking you out to lunch to welcome you to the workplace . . . or to dig for information to use against you so she can swoop in when you get demoted? Did she get passed up for the job you were just offered? Does she have a friend who wanted your job? By doing your homework, you'll be able to separate the true friends who will lift you up from the ones who are wishing you'd fall.

Figuring out the motive behind an action in the workplace can not only help you understand why something is happening and give you perspective, it can also help better prepare you for how to handle the situation. It's one of the pillars in reporting in the field and can help you make decisions in the workplace, too.

Take the case of my agent in Kansas City. He was a bulldog. Fiercely loyal and supportive, he would do anything he could to fight for every penny he thought his clients deserved. Shortly after he completed a contentious back-and-forth negotiation when I was promoted from weekends to weekdays, my boss approached me and suggested I get another agent. One he recommended. His argument was my agent was "mean" and "scary" and that I'd have better success with my career if I hired an agent he had worked with in the past.

It being my boss, the man who spent countless hours going over shows with me, picking them apart, coaching me on how to be a better anchor and reporter, I took his suggestion and hired his friend. Not to mention, we had just inked a very generous (to my 24-year-old brain at least) renegotiation contract. At the time, this seemed like the right thing to do and made sense.

Years later I discovered the agent who was his friend, was his friend of a reason: he was soft on negotiating and didn't stand up for me when I needed advice, coaching, or feedback. It all started to make sense. If my first agent was a fierce tiger, this one was an affable lop-eared bunny. He was hesitant to pick up the phone to call the station if an issue arose, didn't push back nearly as hard as I'd like during contract negotiations, and worst of all, didn't seem 100 percent in love with me and my work. He'd act shocked when I got promotions and at one point told me my work was "pretty good." How could he be my advocate when he thought my work was only pretty good? Here I was, paying him thousands of dollars every month and my agent was more interested in protecting his friends than having my best interests at heart. The last straw was when a reporter friend was talking to a VP of News at a convention and mentioned my agent by name as being "easy." I fired him the next week. In this case, being easy was pretty much the same as being sleazy.

The agent debacle got me thinking: motive is everything. I doubt my mentor was trying to be malicious, but his motive was self-serving. Save the company money. My soft agent was soft because he was friends with all of these employers and was close to retirement age. It's crucial to think about every possible scenario of why someone recommends that you do something. Ask yourself these critical questions: Why would someone want me to do this? Does this person directly benefit somehow if I follow a certain directive? Does he or she have a friend or family member who would? Asking the "why" isn't just for reporters, it's for anyone and everyone with a boss.

DIG DEEPER:
HOW TO DEAL WITH THE PRYING COWORKER

Upon arriving in Kansas City after a short year-long stint in a tiny market in western Massachusetts, I was bright-eyed and bushy-tailed, enthusiastic to be at a prestigious station in a medium-to-large-sized city so early in my career. But shortly after I started, a discrimination lawsuit was filed by three of the senior on-air female talent who felt like they were being pushed out for younger talent like me. In the affidavit and in whispers I'd overhear in the hallways it was clear the older crowd didn't think I belonged or was qualified for the weekend morning anchor position. Truth is, with a year of experience under my belt and never having anchored a day in my life, I wasn't qualified. But it wasn't everyone else's job to judge until I could prove my worth in other ways.

This made me feel alone and depressed. Many of my colleagues were not just a few years older but decades older, and didn't socialize after work, opting to go home and be with their families. This I understood. But it was a stark contrast to my former job, where my coworkers provided me a robust social life with weekly dinners or drinks on the weekends. My new reality was going home by myself many days after my shift, watching episodes of "Barefoot Contessa" on the Food Network and trying to re-create her recipes that never seemed to come out anywhere nearly as perfect as they did on TV.

So, when I received an email from a colleague who was in her late twenties, asking me to lunch, I responded right away with zeal. Yes! At last! A potential friend! Lana had been a reporter in Madison, Wisconsin, and Buffalo, New York, and was relatively new at the game herself. I was about to embark on my first on-air girls lunch date in my new city and was already mentally preparing what to wear.

We met at a popular Midwest chain restaurant that featured unlimited garlic fries, a million flavors of milkshakes, and burgers the size of your head. Over our gargantuan meal, Lana asked me how I liked living in Kansas, how I felt about my colleagues, the boss, and what my career goals were.

At the time, being 23 years old, I just assumed this was basic getting-to-know-you chatter and since I was feeling sadly desperate for female companionship I spilled my guts as if we had known each other for years. When the last of our thick chocolate malts were sucked up, and we stood to leave, I beamed, "Let's do this again!" Lana gave what seemed like an enthusiastic (albeit I should have realized, insincere, like her anchor expressions) affirmation; we hugged and were on with the rest of our day.

When I got back to work the next week, something seemed off. Several weeks passed, and Lana didn't make any effort to reach out, to say she enjoyed lunch with me, or as much as look at me in the newsroom. What happened to our burgeoning friendship? Did I do something wrong? I was crushed.

It wasn't until more than a month later, I learned from Abbie, a producer at the station (who would later become one of my closest friends), that Lana just wanted to dig for information. She had approached Abbie several times baiting her to say something negative about my workplace performance. Example: "So, what did you think of Dion's story on the Hannah Montana concert last night?" (This was way before Miley Cyrus started twerking on stage with Robin Thicke.) "Don't you think her wearing a blonde wig like all those little girls in the crowd is not real journalism?"

She also had mentioned to her in separate conversations that she felt like she deserved to have my position, given that she has seven years' more experience. (Good LORD, I thought. Did everyone want my job?)

It suddenly all made so much sense. Here I was, telling Lana how I wasn't all that keen on my new city, mostly because I didn't know anybody, and that I dreamed of one day becoming an anchor at a top 10 market. A supervisor suspiciously approached me the following week to inquire about my career aspirations and if I had been looking for a job. Since there was only one person I had confessed this to, my heart sank. How could I have been so naive to spill my guts to someone who would betray my trust for their own personal gain?

Ever since the Lana betrayal, I became ultra-mindful when others approached me in person or online to chitchat and ask a few too many questions. Over the years I've honed my tiptoeing skills and deploy strategies to shut down the snoopers so they don't suspect you're suspecting them of being busybodies. Here's what I've learned:

Zip It, Zip It Good

Your goal during these nosy attempts at personal data mining is to give the other person the tactful equivalent of talking to the hand. You want to end their prying while still keeping things civilized. In some relationships you can call the other person out and say, "Hey, are you being nosy?" but chances are, if the person feels the need to pry, it clearly means he or she is not comfortable enough having a straightforward conversation to get the desired information out of you.

A Case for Vague

It's hard to escape a tough question without making a blatant change-of-subject, or in the TV business, a "hard right turn," going from a story about a unicorn festival to a triple homicide. Instead, being obscenely general can not only shut down the questioning but satisfy the other person's need for an answer. Today, when people ask me what my career aspirations are, I tell them I can't think that far ahead into the future because life changes so quickly you never know what's going to happen. Another good response in the form of a vague joke is, "I just want to get through the week. I can't even think about aspiring to anything other than what's for lunch tomorrow!"

Feign Ignorance

Playing dumb sounds terrible, so I like to think of it as playing it smart by "feigning ignorance" to handle certain situations tactfully. A favorite pastime of coworkers wherever you are employed is to gossip and speculate about who is getting fired, who is getting a promotion, who is sleeping with whom, and so forth. By blatantly saying you know nothing of the situation or haven't heard a thing (even if you might have) renders you useless to the other person. In these cases, being useless is a positive.

The Brush-Off

Journalists are extra inquisitive, so whenever someone tries to get me to talk about someone behind their back, or reveal the identity of someone who did something or said something, if I don't want to share, it's as easy as saying, "It's not important" or "Just someone I know." Being prepared with a quick brush-off prevents further digging—even after the "C'mon, you can tell me."

Follow-up question: After deploying any vagueness, ignorance, or the brush-off, the best thing to do is to ask your own question to the other person to shift the focus on cultivating information from you to neutral subjects pertaining to them. By asking a question, it forces the other person to respond and hopefully forget about his or her own probing questions. It then gives you a door to wrap up the conversation and remove yourself from the situation.

End of Story

The last resort is when you encounter someone who just can't stop prying, even after you've done all the feigning ignorance, brushing off, and follow-up questioning. Sometimes you just have to nip it in the bud and tell the other person, "Hey, let's move on" or sometimes I'll say, "No means no" and play it off as a joke. The key is to be just firm enough that the other person understands you're about to be mad if he or she keeps pushing.

LEARN TO TRUST . . .
BY TESTING THE WATERS

Figuring out if three senior anchors/reporters in Kansas City were on my side was pretty easy, since I was clearly named in the affidavit they filed when they sued the station for age discrimination. (I was the much younger woman who was offered an anchoring job over them.) While the women were perfectly kind and professional to my face, I have no doubt they felt I was not entitled to anchor in market number 33 so soon out of college. So, I just steered clear and tried not to ever get in their way.

But in many more instances, it was challenging to crack through the smiling, seemingly friendly facade to determine who would be on my team and who would create an invisible one-sided rivalry. Today, I can usually get a general sense of how our relationship will be within the first three encounters. It's not just determining motive, or using some of the body language cues discussed in the first chapter. Sometimes it takes getting burned first.

The whole concept of testing the waters to protect oneself came after getting badly burned from actual water . . . and a photo of poop.

A Stinky Situation

One day while getting ready for my newscast at a station that shall not be named, I went to the makeup room to de-shine my sweaty, practically reflective forehead when a foul, sewer-like odor wafted through the hallway. It was so puke-inducing I was willing to bet either an animal had somehow gotten inside and died, or someone had a very embarrassing accident after eating too much Mexican food. Turned out a sewer line had burst and begun seeping stench and brown particles all over the tiled floor. After screeching in horror with a meteorologist who happened to be in the room already, semi-trapped by the fast-moving liquid around her, I snapped a photo to document the hilarity of the situation. Since a colleague who worked on my show was out sick that day, I texted him the photo with the caption, "Be glad you are not here to witness the sewer geyser!" A few hours later, the liquid mess was cleaned up, the pipe fixed, and I thought all would be fine in the world.

Except the next day, I woke to a flurry of texts asking if I had seen the news. An industry blogger had obtained the photo of our makeup room mishap and published the story for the whole nation to see. HOW!? None of my friends outside the building knew the photo was taken by me, as there was no attribution or credit on the image. But how did the photo get to the blog? The meteorologist must've told our managers I leaked the photo, because she was in the room with me at the time of the incident and when I snapped the pic. The meteorologist saw me text it to our colleague. Why didn't she defend me and say I took the photo but had sent it to someone else? HR called me into their office shortly after, and I was pegged the mole, even though all I did was send a text.

This experience taught me two things: First, be aware of those you text these seemingly innocent/funny photos to. Second, sometimes it takes a test to determine who is or is not trustworthy.

Years later, when rumors began spreading about various people in the newsroom on a different news blog, I wondered if it was one of the photographers I worked with on occasion. Ted asked a lot of nosy questions and always had a habit of saying, "Whatever is said in the truck stays in the truck" as soon as we stepped inside the vehicle for our assignments. Anybody who feels the need to say this clearly is not keeping what's discussed close to the vest. So, one day after he asked what was happening to an anchor who was out on medical leave and if she was coming back, I purposely let slide a factoid I knew he would find salacious.

"I'm going to be filling in on the show for several weeks."

This was a true statement, yes. But one I normally wouldn't reveal to anyone, as this opens the doors to even more speculation and nosy nellies. "Are you replacing her permanently? Would you want to do that schedule? I wonder if they'll give you a big raise?" I could practically hear the inquisitive minds chattering away behind my back and eventually to my face.

Several weeks later, lo and behold, as if by magic my suspicions about Ted were confounded when several coworkers approached me and said, "So I hear you're going to fill in on the big night show for a while." Bingo. Nobody else except my boss knew I was going to be subbing on the show, so by default Ted was our leaker. From that moment on, nothing could be shared with him and that his little saying about "what stays in the truck" was a load of BS. This kind of testing results in a clear picture of whom you can trust in the workplace. It actually helps you avoid uncomfortable confrontations, like when someone's spilled the beans and he or she gets caught. While my experience with Ted didn't warrant a response because it didn't really affect me one way or another, there are other times when the right response must send a loud and clear message: don't mess with me again (for example, like when someone's actions directly impact your daily duties or block your path to success). And it's best to deliver this message while managing to retain poise, professionalism, and dishing out a little sass at the same time.

Who Calls You?

My former coanchor Reggie was facing an ethics investigation for his relationships with one of his sources for a story. He was under suspension when he called me to relay what really happened. Since we were thick as thieves and had made a pact to always have each other's back (as coanchors should), he confided in me that neither of his current coanchors or fellow on-air teammates even did so much as call or text him to see how he was doing. It broke my heart. "D, the people you can count on are the ones who will attend your funeral." This got me thinking: It's not just attending a funeral. It's the little things. The person who will stay a few minutes late after work helping you figure out the new electronic timesheet system. The administrative assistant who brings you an extra cup of coffee when you're working on a particularly challenging project. For me, I knew I had won over the respect of a seasoned reporter when she offered to share a coveted source with me. These are all signs of whom you can count on when the time comes.

YOUR SKINFOLK AIN'T NECESSARILY
YOUR KINFOLK

My college bestie Iris is an anchor in Syracuse, New York. She comes up with the *best* one-liners and catchy phrases that seem to apply to everything. Before I start any new job, she calls me to say,

"Remember: Eyes and Ears Open; Legs and Mouth Shut!" It's her joking-but-not-really-joking way of reminding me to watch out at all times and don't do stupid things.

One of her favorite phrases is by African American writer and anthropologist Zora Neale Hurston: "All my kinfolk ain't kinfolk!"

It's basic human nature to be attracted to people who seem most like "us." A July 2010 issue of *The Personality and Social Psychology Bulletin* carried a story indicating humans are predisposed to be attracted to those who resemble our parents or ourselves. Sometimes this can work to our advantage—it's one method I use to get interview subjects to open up to me. When they mention they lived in the Midwest, I mention my three years of working in Missouri. The ice storms; finger-licking, fall-off-the-bone barbeque; and lack of ocean are usually our common denominator and make the candidates feel like they are almost talking to a friend.

But when it comes to the workplace and your career, that person with the same ethnic background, haircut, or same level of career experience doesn't mean you'll be viewed as being on the same team.

JUST BECAUSE WE'RE ALL XYZ . . . DOESN'T MEAN WE'RE BFFS

Let's make sure to get this part straight: I believe in professional groups, whether they be for all one ethnic background, or for women or professionals in general. These groups provide a sense of community and support otherwise not found in the workplace. Especially during my non-Asian environment years (this was pre-San Francisco when I lived in Kansas, Charlotte, and Tampa),

I couldn't help but feel a surge of pride in witnessing individuals who looked like me and shared similar struggles thrive in this competitive, sometimes cruel, industry. These conventions essentially felt like several days where the playing field was leveled, and I was no longer the "exotic" or "token" one, but just someone who was seen for her talents, not her skin color and eye shape.

But just because we're cradled in this safe nest/cocoon support-group-like atmosphere doesn't mean you can run your mouth the same as if you were back in college.

There's an amazing Facebook group for females in TV news with about 5,000 members from across the country. The women range from reporters fresh out of journalism 101 to seasoned veterans, producers, and anchors who've worked at five or more television stations in their storied careers. I know that the woman who started this group several years ago intended it to be a place where people with similar backgrounds could seek guidance. She started it when she was working in a small market in Nebraska and struggling with questions nobody seemed able to answer. The purpose of the group was for other TV news ladies to interact, get advice, share their worries and struggles (like how to pay rent and afford work clothes on a $23,000-a-year contract), find jobs, and meet mentors. Women were taking comfort in also sharing their stories getting motivated and inspired for their days of oftentimes hard-hitting, depressing news.

As supportive and incredible as this community was, the worrisome reason why I scaled back on my participation is that women began using the group as a therapy session and forgot about professionalism. Just like how cyber bullies develop screen-courage because nobody can see them in real life, these women suddenly developed the same affliction, except many believed since they were in an invitation-only group, they were part of some exclusive club where whatever is said in the group stays in the group. (Are we in Vegas? I think not!) The group feed was clogged with confessions about hating bosses, their salaries, and details of their agents and contracts. What was shocking was that most used their real names. Even the ones who didn't have profile photos that could, with a little research, reveal their true identities.

My friend who started the group years ago quit cold turkey, tired of the bullying, the name-calling, and out-of-line comments. The forum's intention of being a safe, supportive place had morphed into a place where people felt free to expose their worst sides. An anchor friend in the Pacific Northwest revealed to me later that she was burned when someone took her comments about looking for a job and not only leaked them to a news blog, but went as far as sending an anonymous email to her boss informing him of her job search. A moderator ended up taking over the page and now helps police any inappropriate behavior and fields questions and topics to hide women's identities if they so choose.

If you are ever involved in a group like this—where it's an in-person networking group or something through social media—ask yourself these questions:

- **Who *are* these people?** In a group of 5,000 people, do you know the basics of every single person? Probably not. Why would you share your problems or comments with those whom you don't know basic information about, like the state they live in?

- **Are you getting goodies back?** I jokingly tell my single girlfriends not to give away the goodies if they're not getting the goodies back. (I'll let you interpret this as you wish!)

This also applies to working relationships. If you're driveling on about something yet the other person isn't engaging or blathering back, it's a sign that he or she is not interested, and is possibly just harvesting your information to use down the road.

- **Is this the right time?** Instead of a verbal mudslide right away, can I develop a relationship with someone first, and truly get to know someone before engaging in conversations that reveal facets of my life? Please don't be like the young woman who once trapped me in an elevator at a convention to spill her career woes with me. TMI!

MIND GAMES: WATCH OUT FOR KIKI, THE HUMAN ROADBLOCK TO SUCCESS

Even before I arrived at the station, people warned me about Kiki. At least a dozen fellow journalists in various markets and even one of my mentors in his wise, diplomatic, way, much like white-bearded Dumbledore (the headmaster of Harry Potter's wizarding school) did for his wizards-in-training, imparted these words upon me: steer clear of those who try to get in the way of your success. My agent even said he was prepared to make calls to my management if Kiki ever tried to pull any of her BS.

Kiki was an anchor who had been at the station for nearly two decades and had more than paid her dues moving up the TV market ladder, just as I did.

Surely the rumor of her bullying a younger female on-air talent so badly she had to take medical leave for being so traumatized was an exaggeration.

The first few months were okay. We rarely saw each other, apart from the random hellos in the hallway. But as my profile rose, and I was assigned the big stories that sometimes received national attention, and praise from my managers, she started creeping around my desk, making odd comments. "Did you get a haircut? Oh, you did? Hmm." Or while viewing a photo of me and a friend from a gala I was emceeing, she cooed condescendingly, "What's that? Are you participating in a Miss America pageant?" It was like a line graph: as my on-air time grew and the stories I covered received more attention, ever the more Kiki's friendly exterior began to crack like mud in the sun. If she was on my line graph, the line that represented her underhanded pettiness began to rise alongside my ascent.

One day she even came over to my desk while I was working, deep in the zone on a project that was due in less than 15 minutes, and insisted I listen to what she had to say and that it was important. Without removing my headphones, I looked at her incredulously as if to say, "Really?" and made a gesture to my wrist and tapped my watch face twice.

"No, we need to talk now," she insisted.

I yanked the headphones out of my ears in one downward pull and turned my chair in a semi-circle to face her. Kiki gave me an earnest look and said, "Your anchoring is good but you need to work on your credibility. Take it from me. I was like you when I was young, so it'll eventually come."

Hold up. Did a grown woman, 18 years my senior, really just come over to me unannounced, out of context, and while I was in the middle of trying to make a deadline and school me on how to do my job? What was the purpose of this? An attempt to get me to lose focus? Start doubting myself? What she had just done was so blatantly offensive and uncalled for, there was no way I was going to let her have the satisfaction of affecting me. I was now 12 minutes from deadline and couldn't afford to let this jab bring me down.

Part of why I was able not to lash out at Kiki was because, in addition to many people warning me about her wiley ways, I understood where she was coming from because I had been a version of her in my mid-twenties. I was insecure and felt compelled to assert my dominance toward those whom I deemed threatening. You'll read more about this in Chapter 5, but unlike Kiki, I had figured myself out and why I felt the way I did. Her motive was to stop my upward trajectory by making these kinds of comments. Knowing she was probably dealing with inner turmoil made me feel sorry for her, not sorry for me. Understanding other people's motives for their behavior leads to an understanding of why a particular exchange is happening. Were her comments irritating? Absolutely. But knowing someone's motive allows you to react calmly and forge ahead with little disruption. As a bonus? Remember how our reactions are like a daily performance review? Kiki's treatment of me didn't go unnoticed by the rest of the newsroom. Many would later tell me they were impressed by my resilience and that incident helped build my reputation. It'll ultimately help yours, too.

FEEDBACK: YOU KNOW YOU WANT IT. YOU NEED IT. SOMETIMES YOU HATE IT. SOMETIMES YOU HAVE TO GIVE IT

Email from Mom:

> Number 1 Didi, When I tried open my eyes wide and big, this
> eye movement create lots rankles on my forehead. Thus, I
> always tried not to open my eyes too wide to avoid forehead

rankles. I have seeing you doing it today. (use mirror to see I was correct) I eat too much cabbage today, now stomach has lots gas . . . I got to go drink one tablespoon apple cider vinegar delude with cup water to cure gas. (work well all the time)

MOM

OMG. Staring back at the email I felt the familiar simmering of blood begin to rise to my face. In her all-too-blunt (you'll learn more about that shortly), roundabout broken-English, in a condescending-yet-caring tone only my mom could achieve, she was trying to tell me lines were beginning to appear on my forehead and that I was looking bloated and needed to de-puff with her homemade remedy.

This was my weekly feedback email from my mother in Connecticut who was livestreaming my newscast from her iPad at two o'clock in the morning Eastern Time. It's taken years of training and discipline and soul-searching to get to the point where instead of firing back an aggressive "Ma. What. The. HECK. Is. Wrong. With. You. I am never emailing you back again!" I took a deep breath, right-clicked, and hit "Copy" on the message, and posted her correspondence on Facebook.

This irritating correspondence was the least of my worries. (More on Mom's email later.)

Who knew this constant criticism, the same criticism that drove me nearly to the brink of panic attacks and depression growing up, would serve as a training ground for what was in store for my career? Turns out, not only is the workplace filled with managers, colleagues, and mom-clones, but their critiques could be much more brutal.

Then there are the times you yearn for feedback. Some kind of assessment of how you're doing. In school, your grades serve as evaluation, as do regular check-ins with counselors and professors. But in your career, I'm pretty sure the president of your company has little time to meet about your workplace performance. That is, if he or she even knows about your daily work habits and contributions. And then there are the annual performance reviews where you do get feedback and it doesn't always seem fair. When you do get critiqued, what should you listen to?

While your job may not require you to be on display for hundreds of thousands of viewers each day, you too are always being watched. By your boss. Your peers. Your customers. And along with it, comes feedback. Sometimes unwanted, always thought-provoking, but it should never be taken at just face value. It's how you react to it that can make the difference between a promotion or driving yourself to the brink. Or in my case, a bad case of TMJ from subconscious anxiety combined with nighttime teeth grinding. Let me tell you about one of my favorite experiences receiving feedback.

You vs. the World . . . or Just One Person

When I first got to Tampa Bay, wanting to get ahead of the onslaught of wardrobe suggestions from the impending visit from the clothing consultant, I asked one of my managers if he thought the royal purple dress I was wearing would be appropriate for the anchor desk.

The Milly dress was well-made in a thick ponte fabric and a silky, rich-feeling lining. The sleeves were tiny caps, outlined with black leather trim. It was my recently acquired 90-percent-off-retail-price eBay win, and made me feel like a million bucks. This was just how I wanted to start off the first days of my new job.

Without skipping a beat, my manager said, "Dion, the style's great. Just great for this market. As long as you keep your arms toned."

Did I hear this correctly? The dress was fine, but my arms may be on the brink of not being fine?

Since it was my first week, I made a flexing motion with my biceps and perkily chirped, "See? *So toned!*"

Not wanting to displease my boss, I went on an exercise binge. Kettlebells, dumbbells, and push-ups got incorporated into my routine. More dips! Work those muscles past fatigue and into failure! For months, every single day, my arms went through torture in order to keep them rock hard.

It wasn't until my ultra-toned, strict vegan, personal trainer of a coanchor, donned a sleeveless dress and sat down next to me to prepare for the newscast. I took one glance at the preview monitor in the desk and did a momentary double-take. It was plain to see the contrast. My arms had ballooned to the size of this woman's waist. I had transformed into a female Asian version of The Hulk! (Okay, maybe it wasn't that bad, but it was a huge difference.) My arms had become bulky instead of slim and toned, which is what they were when I first got hired.

When I broached the subject with my bestie, a reporter in Syracuse, she said, "Dion, are you on crack? You're what, like a hundred pounds? Girl, your body looked great just the way it was before!" She proceeded to text me a photo from our last outing together. Yep. She was right.

I felt ashamed. This was one of my closest friends who was proud to be plus-sized, loved her body, and *owned* her look. And here I was, a once self-confident news anchor, turned obsessed exercise lunatic over chiseling my deltoids all because of one man's comment.

That day I made a vow to never let my own judgment be clouded by just one person's comment, let alone a man who did not seem very toned and fit himself. That experience taught me how subjective and complicated comments, critiques, and overall feedback can be, even when they come from an "expert" or person of authority. So as wrong and rebellious as this may sound, here's something to consider: you don't have to listen. Sure, being able to accept feedback can make you more skilled and better at your job. But it can also drive you to the brink of madness and failure . . . or in my case bodybuilder-like arms.

Don't Forget About *You*

Oftentimes in our haste to please the boss or others, we forget to be true to ourselves. I've always been confident in my wardrobe choices (the fact I was featured in *Glamour* for my "work uniform" was probably a good indicator of this) and had no issues with my arms. Not to mention, that purple dress was right in line with what others were wearing anyway. Why was I asking an unfashionable man who wore mom jeans on Fridays (and not in the stylish hipster way, either) if my outfit was appropriate if I already knew the answer?

Gracefully Receive Feedback . . . the Good, the Bad, the Total BS

There are times when you know something is such bad advice you have to just laugh. Like when a makeup artist turned my swivel chair around and, in the mirror, I stared back at a large black fake mole on my upper lip. The artist's recommendation was that I create a signature look like Marilyn Monroe or Cindy Crawford and don a large black eyeliner mole each morning. What if I blew my nose and accidentally wiped off the dot one day? I'd be deemed the freckle fraud! Even at 24, I knew better than to listen to this cockamamie idea! I've made quite a name for myself, without a mole, thank you very much.

But then there are the times when you can glean something useful out of a critique.

When I got to San Francisco, after three years of working in Florida, it was recommended I ease my high-energy anchoring style to something a bit more subdued for the market. In Tampa Bay, the stories were about alligators and meth heads. Management there would come into the studio at 6 p.m. and clap three times chanting, "Energy! Energy! Energy!" to get us to be louder, faster, and more intense so the viewers wouldn't fall asleep. My new Bay Area covered more social issues like protests and tech-world news, which didn't lend itself to that in-your-face style.

This would be a big departure from what I was trained to do in a former life. Re-tuning my entire style wasn't going to be easy. Instead of taking offense to this idea (Why did you hire me if you didn't like how I talked!?), I wanted to explore the idea more before I took the steps to change my anchoring.

Second . . . or Third Opinion

Like getting diagnosed with a disease or some serious medical condition, having another expert weigh in can help put the situation into perspective, and help you decide how to proceed. The key is to do this only with people who are knowledgeable to the situation. Would you ask a NASA scientist how to knit a sweater?

Pick the Right People

Feedback critiquing your performance is a personal issue and, just like sensitive subjects, those second or third opinions should be from those you trust. The last thing you want is for your colleagues to play a game of telephone or start rumors that management is unhappy with your work. When it comes to my job, I trust my former coanchor, a former investigative reporter, and my agent. They know the business and don't work with me, and I know will shoot me straight.

Get on the Same Page

In the example above, since all of my trusted confidants agreed that relaxing my delivery wouldn't hurt, and could only potentially help, I gave it a shot, slowing down my sentences and not embellishing dramatic events as much. These people helped me understand that this feedback wasn't because I lacked skill or talent. I just needed to adapt to my new surroundings, while still being me.

GIVE FEEDBACK: THE RIGHT WAY

Talk show superstar Oprah Winfrey spent many years in local television before propelling into the network TV stratosphere. What would have happened if she had listened to that silly TV producer in Baltimore who called her "unfit for television" and she quit? When I was leaving Kansas City, a manager told me it would take "5, 10, 20 years before you'll become an evening anchor." At the time I was crushed, but knew this wasn't true, as stations had already been pursuing me for various roles other than mornings. Had I listened to this absurdity and not applied for these positions, I wouldn't have, the very next month, accepted a job offer as evening anchor in Charlotte, North Carolina.

At about that time, the tables started turning and I was the one getting requests to provide feedback to others. This wasn't only from my teammates who suddenly saw me as having a valuable opinion, but young reporters messaged me regularly, asking for a critique of their demo reels and insight into what career path to take. What I discovered, from being bombarded with a myriad of suggestions and feedback myself, was that reviewing a person's work is a great responsibility. What you recommend can have a lasting effect on someone's psyche and career.

- **Digestibility:** A well-known plastic surgeon once asked me to critique his latest on-camera interview and I tore it to shreds. Not in a mean or abrasive way, but that I didn't leave any stone unturned. From his outfit to body posture, his speech delivery, and content. It was too much for him to digest and he ended up getting overwhelmed. His next interview was even more riddled with long-winded answers and a sweaty brow. People can only handle one or two suggestions at a time. Too many comments can give the impression that they're not good at the task at hand and end up demotivating the person. Perhaps if I had given him just a few notes, we would have seen improvement from the doc, not a worse performance.

- **Follow Through with an Example:** Pairing the one or two suggestions with an anecdote or explanation not only adds gravity to your tips but also helps the person understand why it is important. When I suggested a cub reporter get rid of her handheld microphone in favor of a wireless one, I explained it would not only make her on-air presence more natural, but also allow her to be more active, demonstrative, and creative. Then I showed her two clips of me, one holding a microphone and one without. I think she got the hint because in the next demo she sent me, she was 10 times more relaxed and conversational in her delivery.

- **The Only Person Who Can Make That Decision Is You:** This is always my disclaimer when providing feedback. Why? Because giving someone guidance with a definitive answer isn't fair. When I was debating between three different jobs as I left Kansas City, one mentor said, "Take the job that pays the most!" Sure, that job probably paid a third more than the other two options, but it wasn't the role I wanted to be in, or in a city where my husband and I wanted to live. There are so many things to take into consideration, that a more fleshed-out response with the pros and cons of each job and each city would have been more helpful. In the end, only I could make the decision on how my career would shape up.

PS: As for my mom's email? While it may seem cruel and unusual to post her words on the World Wide Web for all to see, it's actually turned into entertainment and a big part of my personal brand. One day, out of frustration, I shared a drawing she had sketched, took a photo of, and emailed to me in between the 6 and 11 p.m. newscasts. It was a primitive ballpoint pen drawing of my head with some strands of hair flipping out to one side and an arrow pointing at the misplaced hairs. I laughed so hard at this tiny cartoon version of me, there was no time to be annoyed. So, I posted the photo on Facebook, and my audience loved it. As the dozens and dozens of comments and "likes" amassed, I realized my fans appreciated the fact that the seemingly put-together lady on TV has a crazy mom, too. At the same time, my mom would see my Facebook post and understand I got her message loud and clear. This may not be a conventional way to talk to your mother, but at least she gets a kick out of the viewers who think she's funny and adorable. Everybody wins.

The Matt Lauer Effect
Intelligent Courage

What I know for sure is that speaking your truth is
the most powerful tool we all have.
—OPRAH WINFREY, Golden Globes 2018

WE'VE ALL READ the headlines. Matt Lauer. Harvey Weinstein. Charlie Rose. Women are finally feeling more comfortable with talking about sexual harassment and assault . . . but it still keeps happening. When something is a well-kept secret, or you're going up against a superior, how do you find the courage and strength to stand up and do something without fearing retaliation or being branded a liar? Taking it a step further, how do you tackle the monumental task of changing workplace culture?

By speaking out the right way, that's how.

Whether dealing with sexist comments or full-on sexual harassment and assault, remember: you're not alone. A 2018 survey by the nonprofit Stop Street Harassment found just over 80 percent of women had experienced sexual harassment in one form or another during their lifetime. Just as there are degrees of inappropriateness, there are different ways to handle each situation.

BABY WEINSTEIN

The first time a male made a sexist and inappropriate comment to me was in the third grade, by a boy named Ross. I remember it like it was yesterday. Ross had greasy, sandy blonde hair, buck teeth, and a pig-like nose and wore round shiny gold glasses with a double bridge before it was the hipster, trendy thing to do.

While my eight-year-old self didn't know the word "racist," I knew he was not a good person for the icky way I felt when he stretched his eyes into two slits and called me "Wing Wong Ding Dong." I didn't know the word "sexist," but knew saying things about my looks, other girls' looks, and our 20-something-year-old teacher Ms. Karnow's looks was wrong.

To deal with Ross, my underdeveloped child brain used the first and only response instinct it knew: violence. Since I didn't want to touch the slimeball (boys were *so* gross), I would eat my lunch and use the plastic baggie that held my sandwich as a glove/barrier to pinch Ross on various parts of his body until he started screaming.

Ross must've been into sadism because not only did he seem to enjoy being punished, this never solved a thing. He'd come back to school the very next day, with renewed enthusiasm and even more remarks and actions like telling me he loved me, I was sexy, and he wanted to marry me. All of this, of course, made me feel continually uncomfortable. How does an eight-year-old know the word "sexy" anyway? After a year of fending off this kiddy perv, he thankfully moved away.

Twenty-eight years later, it turns out the world is full of Ross's who can't be stopped with a plastic baggie and workplace violence. They're also a hundred times worse.

By now, you know all about Mario Batali, Les Moonves, Kevin Spacey, and the multitude of famous, powerful men who've fallen from grace because of their alleged actions. The *New York Times* even published an article in 2017 naming 71 high-profile men to fall from power following the Harvey Weinstein uncovering . . . and that number only represents the ones we know about. #MeToo is just as strong today as it was when it first gained momentum after actress-turned-activist Alyssa Milano made the call to action in the fall of 2017 for women to start speaking out about their experiences using the hashtag on Twitter. The idea is strength in numbers. Remarkable shows of strength and solidarity have emerged since #MeToo was formed, and not just from the millions of Tweets. You've got "Silence Breakers" like Adama Iwu, a lobbyist who rallied about 150 women to speak out about their experiences with sexual harassment after she was victimized herself, and Janete Perez, who co-led the Women's March in San Francisco and rallies for females to vote to make their voices heard. But how do we turn those Tweets into action . . . and ultimately widespread change?

STAND UP IN STEPS

During my entire career, spanning six cities (five on-air), whenever I told a coworker or friend about something that made me feel like I did in third grade with Ross Bronstein all over again, the immediate response was "Go to HR," or "You gotta tell the boss." But I was petrified to do so, not wanting to ruffle any feathers or be pegged as a complainer. You may have a similar feeling if you are going through this in your own workplace.

Growing up in a Chinese household where stamina and tolerance were two of the most admired qualities in a person, I figured I could avoid these offenders and push the incidents under the rug.

But then there was Liam.

Liam was the jovial fill-in anchor whose quick and clever quips and uncanny talent of impersonating anybody in an instant made him a fan favorite and a fun and likable colleague. He was always one to stop by the desk of a new employee to make small talk and genuinely seemed interested in whatever the other person had to say. Too bad his lightning-quick wit also applied to his inappropriate comments and the way his sparkling hazel eyes would sometimes scan my body as if to mentally undress me.

There were a lot of things about our working relationship I liked. When I was new, and he was assigned a big-name interview, he'd offer it to me first in an effort to help build my credibility in the market. He would nominate me for special assignments, which the other on-air talent coveted. He had a down-to-earth quality I liked in a desk partner (AKA his ego wasn't the size of Texas), and I also enjoyed how dorky he was in his efforts to be "cool," like referring to himself in the third person as "Rad Man" despite his black orthopedic shoes and pleated pants. Bottom line: he felt like a friend. Just a really perverted one.

It was these things that allowed me to let slide the barrage of inappropriateness. His excessive and deliberate use of the word "penetration" during conversation or blatant breast-staring. But the last straw for me revolved around his audio earpiece cord.

Liam and I had just completed a newscast and were headed down the hall into the newsroom when I noticed he was twirling his earpiece cord (in the business, it's called an IFB cord and helps us hear our producer) like a Valley Girl twirling a strand of hair. He seemed to be in a good mood, so I joked wagging my finger in the air and moving my neck side to side and said:

"Liam, don't you be twirling that cord at me!"

His response was unexpectedly bad, even by Liam standards, and caused me to nearly stumble on the perfectly flat carpet.

"Oh, trust me, I have something much bigger and longer I could be twirling around you . . . in your face."

The blood drained from my face and I looked away in an attempt to hide my disappointment and horror. What was I supposed to do? There were a million things I wanted to say but for some reason my brain and mouth were frozen in time. A horrifying image of what he was insinuating seared itself into my head. Instead of words forming in my throat, all that came out was an awkward dry cough/laugh and I robotically made an excuse of needing to go back to the makeup room to retrieve my hair spray.

For a week, I contemplated what to do, confiding in only two women: one a trusted assignment desk manager and the other, one of the longest-tenured technical behind-the-scenes engineers in the entire city. Both had told me numerous stories of working as the first female in their field in the 1960s, 1970s, and 1980s. Can you imagine being called "little girl" day after day by your coworkers . . . even though you're a nearly six-foot-tall woman? Or never being assigned to cover presidential visits or history-making stories because your boss thought females were too emotional while "on the rag" and "belonged in the kitchen, not on Air Force One"?

Both women were very different people but had their own ways of handling injustices in the workplace. One was able to compartmentalize and soldier through instead of letting it get the best of her, which motivated her to stand up for herself and everyone around her. The other would storm into her supervisor's office and not be afraid of the retaliation that could possibly follow because she was so confident in who she was and had such a robust life outside of the workplace she didn't need anybody to like her. (Between you, me, and the lamppost, I think her rumored seven-figure inheritance also probably gave her verbal courage.) As different as these women were, the one thing I admired about both of them, was how they gave zero f**ks.

But I was not ready to act in either of these manners. Compartmentalizing would drive me crazy and probably lead to a mental breakdown. And, I wasn't about to storm into my manager's office and tattle because my boss was always in a state of busy—and unlikely to listen to my problem.

Their varying viewpoints resulted in the realization that (A): There is no one-technique-solves-all kind of fix because every situation is different. There are so many factors—your relationship with the offender, how inappropriate the offense. And (B): You don't have to make a beeline to your human resources, because often it's not necessary and you *can* take matters into your own hands to start.

So, the next day after revealing my story to my female colleagues, Liam and I were discussing our bucket lists and I shared that on mine was to visit a kangaroo farm in Australia. Of course, he made a comment about how I'd fit right in as a "saucy Aussie in a bikini on Bondi." (Honestly, how did he come up with this lame stuff?) I said in the same playful tone, "Liam, if you keep up this #MeToo business, a shark is going to attack you while snorkeling on the Great Barrier Reef." He seemed amused and impressed at my equally quick pun, while all getting my message loud and clear. He never made an uncomfortable comment ever again, and we're still friends to this day.

I call the approach I used with Liam "tone matching." The reason why this approach works is that I got Liam's attention by matching his tone but coupling it with a message completely different than his own. Later on, I'll talk about mirroring someone else's body language and demeanor to get people to open up and talk to you. But tone matching isn't so much physical as it is about volume, manner, content, and feel. Because Liam had an impish delivery of his lame one-liners, I matched the off-the-cuff, casual tone with a serious message. The result is attention-grabbing because of its unexpectedness. The matching of someone's same tone also diffuses the situation just enough where the other person doesn't become defensive or offended.

ESCALATION AND STRENGTH IN NUMBERS

Fortunately, Liam was the best possible example of dealing with someone who needed to be put in his place. He understood right away when I hinted his behavior wasn't appropriate and didn't let it affect our working relationship. But you won't always be this lucky.

One of the events that really made an impact on how I wanted to use my voice in the workplace was hearing Dr. Christine Blasey Ford testify in real time what she alleged Supreme Court Justice Brett Kavanaugh did to sexually assault her at a high school party. Her vivid account of that summer day in 1982 gave me chills, and opened my eyes to what bravery it took for her to speak out. The media were ushered into a separate holding facility after Dr. Ford began receiving death threats. Her husband had to stay home with their children out of fear for their safety. Women from both sides of the aisle (although there were many, many more in support of her than skeptics) came from as far away as Europe to throw support behind the #IBelieveChristine movement. This was an historic moment in time, and I felt a surge of pride being among so many strong, vocal women who rallied behind one of their own.

This national news story reminded me of a situation when applying the Liam Strategy wasn't enough. A relatively new coworker texted me in a panic, asking if I could meet her outside because of an incident she had with a male colleague. I dropped everything I was doing and rushed toward the exit. There, I found my usually strong, outspoken, unshakable (even in times of the most stressful breaking news) producer, Kenya, shaking. She told me in-between dry half-sobs that one of our male associates, Pablo, had accused her of sleeping her way to a promotion. She told me she witnessed him making off-color remarks to interns and gestures that referenced women with large breasts. But him accusing her of spreading her legs instead of putting in hard work and dedication to her job was disgusting and the last straw.

"Dion, I have to say something this time. This has to stop. But what am I supposed to do? Nobody's going to believe me if I tell management. I'm just a producer . . . and I'm still kinda new."

Right then and there I decided it was time for me to speak up, too. For months I had either heard directly or via secondhand of Pablo's infantile exploits. He'd approach women from behind and give them a big bear hug and lift them up off the ground, or massage their shoulders. Another colleague had said she felt "gross" after he made a comment comparing the chests of two female anchors at competing stations and calling it the "Curvy Girl

Olympiad." (Honestly, this was just as bad as Liam's lame nicknames.) It wasn't as though I didn't try to put an end to his sick-
ening behavior, it's just that he seemed impervious to any kind of
hint or clue that his actions were making others feel uncomfortable. The Liam Strategy I had deployed with such success years
earlier fell upon deaf ears. Pablo would defensively brush off my
words of caution and then do it again a day later. So, right then and
there, squished between someone's minivan and hidden behind
a prickly bush with my coworker who was on the brink of a panic
attack, I decided to use my voice to give strength to hers.

To say we were nervous about approaching our boss about a
long-tenured, very popular, decorated member of our workforce
would be an understatement. We knew in order to be taken seriously, not pegged as complainers, or experience backlash for being "tattlers," we had to be methodical in our approach. Here was
our strategy to make a potentially uncomfortable experience safe
and empowering.

- **Find the Numbers:** We knew, just as I had offered to share
  my experiences about Pablo, that if other women were
  to confirm our accusations, it would give us fortitude.
  Chances are, if you've experienced or witnessed unbecom-
  ing behavior that had no place in the workplace, others
  have too. But it's not as though you can send an anonymous
  survey to your peers asking if they've experienced anything pervy with Danny the executive assistant. So, in the
  subsequent weeks, we spent some time testing the waters,
  dropping vague hints with other women at work who may
  have had icky encounters with Pablo. If the topic of, say,
  the Kardashians came up in conversation, I'd make a casual comment about how, "I hate it when people compare

women's butts to those sisters. It makes me feel like raw meat." The comment would then prompt anyone else who felt the same way—because Pablo was the comparer—to reveal that fact. Finding a way to affirm you're not the only one is the beginning of making change.

- **Let Others Do the Heavy Lifting:** Once we found a few women who also experienced this kind of treatment from Pablo, we didn't ask them to speak out. We knew that if we did, word would ultimately get around the newsroom and we'd be pegged as the informants and be branded with scarlet letters for the rest of our working days. Instead, we knew in an HR investigation, our boss would ask who else may have experienced the same unsavory behavior. Since we had already found others, all we had to do was suggest some names and let the company take care of the rest.

- **Stay on Topic:** Pablo had other bad habits, like blowing his nose right before the backrubs, or turning in half-assed assignments at the very last minute. We wanted to talk about those issues as well, but we knew that if we were to veer off topic, our main message of getting him to stop his sexist ways would be diluted. Plus, bad hygiene wasn't an HR violation and mentioning it just gives off the impression that we were complaining.

- **Your Convictions *Are* Valid:** Others will question or even flat-out discredit what you saw, heard, and or experienced. These voices can make you second-guess your convictions. They can even plant questions in your own mind of the turn of events. There were so many people who loved Pablo. Were Kenya and I overreacting? We combed through every single interaction to validate our feelings and came to the conclusion: absolutely *not*. With every iota of my being, I promise you—how you feel dictates the truth every time. Don't let anybody ever take that away from you. Turns out, when you're strong and steadfast in your feelings, others will realize it too. HR acted quickly to launch and complete their investigation and suspended Pablo for two weeks. Pablo never showed anyone a photo of former Playboy Playmates ever again.

STAND UP: FOR YOURSELF AND OTHERS . . . EVEN IF THEY'RE NOT THERE

Part of winning the fight on sexism when it feels like the cards are stacked against you is making the change happen not just for yourself but on behalf of other women in your workplace. A few months ago, my college roommate, Seema, sent me a text message. She explained she had done some attic cleaning and unearthed her journals from our Emerson days. Accompanying the text was a photo. The image was a shot of two lined journal pages. The loopy, semi-cursive handwriting read: "Dion is so dense. She only cares about herself and didn't stand up for me when Cecily called me a slut."

I burst into a nonstop five-minute fit of laughter. Seema and I had done some crazy things in college (including dumpster diving for leftover pizzas) and have since morphed into somewhat responsible adult friends who put our underdeveloped-college-brain years behind us.

Reading those two lines reminded me why it was so important to stand up for others, even when they're not present. Or, as I discovered later on in my career, defending others and going to bat for them are necessary to have a harmonious workplace. Because in my book (no pun intended) if you witness something unscrupulous and don't do anything, you're nearly as bad as the offender.

Standing Up for Someone Else Is Standing Up for Everyone, Including Yourself

It was the story of the month: the massive Kilauea volcanic eruption in Hawaii. Much of my newsroom was mesmerized by the bright orange lava flows invading the Leilani Estates on the big island, and openly wondered where residents had fled to, or when the bubbling magma would cease. Some of my colleagues, however, were more interested in commenting on the woman reporting the story.

For nearly three weeks, my friend Drea was on the front lines as twisting, furious fire-hot lava swirled only a few hundred feet away. Based in Los Angeles, Drea was a network correspondent who sometimes traveled more weeks out of the month than she was at home. She was a versatile reporter who could find herself camped outside a "house of horrors," where children were being chained up in the basement one week, and then behind the scenes on a Cirque du Soleil trapeze the next. During her assignment in Hawaii, we saw her every afternoon and evening, clad in shorts, T-shirt, and ball cap doing hits for the network news and any affiliates around the country who wanted a live reporter in their show.

For 18 days, while Drea covered the lava creep, I heard the same comments from my colleagues. These were not the comments of "Nice job," or "What a trooper, look at how close she is to the lava." Instead, the comments were about her appearance.

"Tell Drea to eat a sandwich. *No*, a cheeseburger, and make it a double!"

"Drea's going to get sucked up by that lava—she's so skinny!"

"Since when does Skeletor report the news?"

By Day 8, I couldn't stay silent anymore. (In hindsight, I should have interjected by Day 1.) Turning to my heavyset male colleague, I blurted, "Hey. What if someone commented on your own daughter's or your wife's weight?"

Undeterred, he said nonchalantly, "Well, nobody's commenting on her weight. I'm commenting on Drea."

Sigh. Deaf ears. Didn't anybody else find the irony in the fact that this commenter was significantly overweight?

As frustrating as this was, I felt confident that I had made my point and at least everyone who was nearby knew my stance on commenting on women's bodies.

The very next day, a different coworker, this time a woman, made a similar comment as soon as Drea appeared on the screen. Instead of commenting on her stellar reporting, her hard work, or her stamina, this particular offender said, "She probably has an eating disorder."

I had it. Now a woman was body shaming another female, setting the example to everyone in the room that this was allowable in our workplace. When no one interjects to say these types of remarks are not okay, these comments become tolerable and the norm. This is how company cultures are shaped—as long as you have a voice, your moral responsibility is to use it. Breaking from my usually composed exterior, I blurted out, "Did we forget she's an amazing reporter?"

My coworkers looked slightly taken aback by my outburst. No one made a peep. (Though one woman rolled her eyes and started furiously typing away, probably to instant message the person next to her to call me a "bitch.") That was that, and we went about our day.

While it may not have seemed this way on the outside, the best thing to come out of that exchange was the silence. This is because the silence wasn't replaced by any more mentions of Drea's or anybody's body from there on out. Even though I could have, I purposely chose not to mention that Drea ate like a sumo wrestler, because addressing her eating habits just shone more attention on her body size instead of her skills and hard work. My reputation remained intact, and as a bonus, defending someone who wasn't even in the room showed others who were bothered by the comments that they had an ally. Sometimes your greatest strength is giving a voice to others who have their own but just aren't there to use it.

TO HR OR NOT TO HR. NOT ONLY IS THAT THE QUESTION . . . BUT *HOW* DO YOU HR?

My first on-air job was during my senior year of college at a tiny television station in Springfield, Massachusetts, in the western part of the state. Thanks to some strategic class scheduling, I was able to complete my final semester at Emerson by lumping my classes into two days, so I could do the 180-mile roundtrip from Boston to Springfield four days a week to work as a reporter. Being 21 years old, I was young and hungry and ready to do just about anything in television news for my barely-over-minimum-wage contract. (Let's just say I made more money as a cashier working overtime at the local grocery store at age 16.)

If a rookie reporter is nicknamed a cub, I was a fetus. My eyes weren't even open to the working world and my lack of experience showed from the rambling, nearly incoherent news stories I cobbled together to the actions I took in the workplace when dealing with others and handling conflict. This was most evident by my penchant for going to HR for reasons that should have been handled by my manager or on my own: An annoying coworker who would inadvertently whistle all day long because of a gap in her front teeth. Wanting to know when I'd get a promotion. (Uhm, I had only been there a piddly six months. Who did I think I was?) Heck. If a peanut butter and jelly sandwich had grape jelly instead of strawberry preserves, I'd probably make a beeline to human resources to have the issue fixed.

Clearly these are not reasons to go running to human resources.

HR's purpose is to protect the company. To act in the best interest of the employer. To make sure labor laws are met and that benefits (and consequences) are doled out appropriately. What I was doing was using HR as my sounding board, punching bag, and occasional therapist. I was a human and to me this was the resource they should be providing. That train of thought got me in a lot of hot water. By aimlessly discussing the gripes I had with my boss combined with issues that served no purpose for the greater good, I was seen as a problem child. But there are times when HR can be your ally, and this is especially true in the #MeToo era. So, when is it appropriate to get human resources involved?

- **Baby Steps Up the HR Ladder:** Think of dealing with uncomfortable situations like climbing a ladder. Human resources is at the very top. Can you solve the issue on the lowest rung without getting anybody involved? If not, do you have a manager or someone whom you can bounce the subject off of to get input? That superior may end up taking the issue to HR on your behalf. If you feel like you're not getting any answers, then maybe it is time to pay that man or woman in the office upstairs a visit.

- **Phrase It So *You* Are Not the Problem:** The job of human resources is to keep the company running smoothly and prevent any legal woes against the top management and senior employees. The last thing HR wants to hear is you complaining about someone without a valid reason to. Over-complainers are miserable people, which sends a message that you're despondent. Your sentences shouldn't start with an "I" because "I want" or "I can't stand" is a reflection on *you*, not how the issue is affecting the company as a whole. Instead, center the complaint about a person and how he or she affects your workflow and contributions to the company.

- **Just the Facts:** The idea of talking to HR can be intimidating. Here's someone (or sometimes two people) staring at you as you're reliving traumatic events, taking notes and possibly recording your every word. Convey just the facts and what is necessary for your team to build their case. You want your side to be heard loud and clear, and not get bogged down with other unnecessary extras.

WHAT DID YOU JUST CALL ME?
(MY NAME IS DION, AND *ONLY* DION)

Years ago, I worked with a meteorologist who perpetually called the women he worked with (including me) "Hon." Jason was born and raised in the Midwest (and still wore cowboy boots) and called women "Ma'am," men "Sir," and the females he was close to "Hon" or "Babe." However, just because he was from the Midwest, didn't make it okay. This was work. Sure, to Jason this was a term of endearment, as we were all good friends. But I'm not his mom, sister, or girlfriend. At work, we were equal.

Indra Nooyi, the CEO of Pepsi, condemned the use of these kinds of pet names in the workplace, saying it's all about dignity. She spoke at a Women in the World Summit and addressed the crowd: "We've got to be treated as executives of people rather than 'Honey,' 'Sweetie,' or 'Babe.' That has to change."

That quote resonated with me, because she was right. Why should women be called nicknames that are meant to describe babies, Goldendoodle puppies, and girlfriends? Would you ever call your male counterpart, "Sexy," "Hottie," or "Boy" during a company-wide meeting?

For almost two years, I let this go on. Jason had good intentions. We were friends! But the last straw broke when I was speaking to a group of college students visiting the station. Here I was, talking about my journey in TV news, moving from city to city every year and being a strong minority role model to these young adults, yet I was being called a pet name as if I were a subordinate, not a hard-working woman who made just about the same salary as this man with 10 more years' experience.

In a joking way, I sassed back, "C'mon Rockstar, none of that. You can't call me 'Hon' at work!" He held up his hands in mock protest and said, "Yes, ma'am! 10-4" and we were good. Just like that. Until a fellow female in the newsroom, Charity, chimed in, "But I *like* it when he calls me 'Hon'!" In an instant, it was all undone. Out the window. K'boshed. Kaput. One step forward, two steps back. Her affirmation that she enjoyed being called "Hon" just undid the progress I had made on behalf of all the women at the station.

Because we had mutual respect for each other, Jason followed my wishes and from that point on, I was "D" or "Dion." It didn't affect our working relationship or our personal relationship one iota. The same couldn't be said for anyone else (including Charity), as everyone, including our assistant news director, was on the receiving end of a few of his "Hons," but I'm nonetheless proud of standing my ground—albeit late. At least I had the gumption, the chutzpah, and courage to take a step at all.

- **Set Precedent:** If you let someone call you "Babe" for two years, you've already set the precedent that it's okay because you haven't done anything about it. What the Jason experience taught me was to shut down future pet names sooner than later. When an older, male assignment desk manager called me "Girl," I cleared my throat and said loudly for the entire newsroom to hear, "I am a woman, Brian. A woman!" He apologized shortly after and never called me "Girl" again.

- **Constant Reminders:** It'll take a while to break someone completely of a longtime bad habit. Brian may have tossed "Girl" out the window, but other pet names would pop out unexpectedly (and I really do believe unintentionally). Since I had already shut him down once, all it took was a gentle reminder why an inappropriate epitaph wasn't acceptable at work for him to stop. The last time he did it, all it required was for me to give him "the look" and from then on, my name was only Dion.

Sexual harassment may be ubiquitous in the workplace, but by learning how to deal with it in a professional and considered manner, you can make huge strides toward changing that for yourself and for other women. The next time you or a colleague are on the receiving end of an inappropriate comment, remember that you have power—you just need to use it in a considered way to achieve your ultimate goal of being treated with respect, as a valued member of your company.

Survival Speak
Talking Your Way Through
the Daily Minefield

OU'RE SPEAKING IN front of a crowd of 300 distinguished lawyers, making a pitch about why they should donate big bucks to support a nonprofit campaign with your company. Because you have three different presentations to three different groups this week, you forget which crowd you're in front of, and you call them the wrong organization. How do you talk yourself out of looking like a doofus? How about those times your manager asks you a question in a department meeting about something you have no idea about? Is there a way to sound intelligent and authoritative when you have no facts or a plan for what to say? What about when you're at a convention, trying to meet the general manager of your work but you're too intimidated to initiate a conversation? And what do you do when what you're listening to is so boring that you can barely stay awake?

These scenarios are just the beginning and are where survival speak comes in. Reporters in the field use it every single day. The ability to talk your way through any scenario with the poise and confidence of a seasoned orator is surprisingly easy, and I promise you can do it, too.

In the movie *Catch Me If You Can*, a young Leonardo DiCaprio plays Frank Abagnale, Jr., a con man with a quick tongue and even quicker wit, which he uses to talk himself into—and out of—sticky situations. With not much education but a lot of street smarts and the ability to think on his feet, this con man morphs into an airline pilot, and then into an attorney, and even a doctor.

While Frank uses his social skills to commit fraud and spends time in prison, he now uses those same skills as a consultant and lecturer for the FBI. The right speaking tips can also get you out of sticky situations, like making that verbal mix-up or adapting to a room full of people you have little in common with.

People who have mastered "survival speak" are pros at reading emotions and instantly switching gears to control the conversation. It's how we reporters get people to let us into their lives, into crime scenes, and into giving us the scoop. Most recently, I used a variation of survival speak to bypass a dozen security guards and gain access into the risers on the Oscars red carpet to take photos of J. Lo, A-Rod, and Lady Gaga . . . without the proper media credentials. (Shhh. Don't tell the Academy.) In the competitive world of television media, getting those photos is a form of survival!

By reading others' emotions and reactions, learning how to listen better, and interacting fearlessly with anybody and everybody, you'll be a valuable asset in every situation. You can have the best Ivy League education and a corner office filled with awards and accolades, but if you can't figure out how to talk about anything with anyone, you've got nothing.

THE REAL-LIFE SOCIAL NETWORK
(BECAUSE VIRTUAL IS *NOT* REALITY)

I know this is going to sound pathetic, but I have to share my dirty little secret. For years, whenever I had to attend a networking mixer, fundraising gala, or awards banquet by myself and had to socialize with total strangers, make small talk, remember names, and sound intelligent, I freaked out. As soon as I picked up my name tag, I would make a beeline for the restroom, lock myself in a bathroom stall, and kill time by checking what was trending on Twitter or playing Text Twist for at least half an hour.

This was my sad ritual to avoid the awkward conversations and ensuing anxiety—the ones where I had to talk about something totally outside my realm of knowledge, or meet people with whom I clearly had no chemistry.

Some people have a fear of flying or public speaking. My fear was socializing in large groups with people I didn't know.

It took dozens of therapy sessions to fully realize that much of my fear stemmed from my childhood, as one of the very few Asian kids in predominantly white communities. Midland, Michigan, where I lived from age 3 to 10, had an Asian population of .04 percent. My middle and high school years were spent in Killingworth, Connecticut, where the Asian population was even more dismal at .01 percent. (Do the math: .01 percent of a population of 6,400 means my mom, dad, and I made up practically the entire demographic.) I was the oddball who brought weird foods to school: dried seaweed snacks instead of Cheetos and these weird sandwiches made with shelf-stable dried pork-floss on steamed bread called *mantou*. (Go figure, today you can find *mantou* on trendy menus as steamed bun sandwiches with pork belly or duck confit stuffed inside. I didn't know it at the time, but I was ahead of the foodie curve!)

It wasn't the lack of diversity that got to me, but rather the never fitting in. Even the other two Asian kids (who were both adopted into Caucasian households) knew how to look and sound like everyone else. While kids at school donned the New England uniform—pink khaki shorts with tiny whales embroidered on them, a polo with an embroidered horse (What was up with all that embroidery?), and Sperry Topsider boat shoes, or the alternate skater look that included items from Hot Topic—my wardrobe consisted of my much-older brother's leftover hypercolor T-shirts (Hey, those are considered "vintage" and highly collectable now!) or dorky overalls from Goodwill. These weren't even the good Salt-N-Pepa stonewashed denim overalls, but the corduroy variety that were in the discount bin after sitting on the rack for one-too-many seasons.

Even though it's been decades since my school years, I remember as clear as day what it was like walking into the lunchroom, feeling everyone's eyes on me, feeling judged, and then wanting to hide in a corner because there was no table I belonged to. I trained myself to be on the lookout for the stares and "side-eye." As soon as I sensed it happening, I would slowly slink out of the cafeteria to eat my lunch somewhere else . . . usually the stairwell or some rarely used hallway where nobody would see how lame and lonely I was.

This is the feeling I would later get whenever I had to enter a big room full of people as an adult.

YOU'VE GOT THIS

I know. This all sounds preposterous, coming from the lady on the TV who talks for a living and socializes in big groups all day long—today I attend and speak to strangers at an average of more than 30 events a year. But it wasn't until I was forced to emcee and host these events that I began to understand how to work these social situations. I learned how to keep a conversation going.

Don't get me wrong, I still hide out in the restroom . . . but now just for a few minutes to fix my hair or makeup and mentally prepare to face the masses.

So, before you decide to skip that next workshop because you won't know anyone and your significant other, colleague, or friend isn't able to join you, rest assured that this chapter will guide you through any social situation and help you learn to socialize like a pro.

FIND AN IN, *ANY* IN.
MEET ANYONE AND EVERYONE

There is something to be said about people who can adapt to whatever situation they find themselves in. They read emotions and can instantly switch gears to control the conversation. Much of my professional success comes from knowing how to use my social currency to read other people's emotions and reactions, instantly assess my interactions with others, and shift gears seamlessly to suit the situation.

I can't stand "conversation starters." They're so forced. You know, those little cards with questions on them, or prompts like, "What is your favorite color?" or "What was the last vacation you took?" They are so inauthentic and unnatural. Who goes up to people in real life and asks questions that don't usually come up in conversation?

Most people already had the basics of conversation starters down, like "What do you do?" or "Where did you grow up?" and

"How long have you worked at the company?" But nobody ever talks about how to meet the person you want to talk to in a more organic, memorable way.

This is where finding the "in" comes in. I started using this technique while reporting in the field to get what we call "person on the street" sound bites in television. This is when you approach a random stranger and ask him his personal feelings about a story. When you're crunched for time, you learn quickly how to get someone to talk . . . and also what'll get you shot down faster than a bad pick-up line.

Sometimes the standard, "Hey, can I ask you a question?" approach works. Sometimes the person is skeptical, but more often than not he or she is caught off guard by this random stranger with exceptionally white teeth and helmet hair approaching with a microphone. Now is time for the "in." It's a question or comment that softens the first interaction with the person so he or she will agree to talk to you on camera. Then you can ease into the questions you really want to ask.

FIND COMMON GROUND
THROUGH STATING THE OBVIOUS

One of the very first stories in my career was about a highly publicized dispute at a school board meeting. My producer sent me out to a local shopping plaza (Yes, this is hard-hitting small-town reporting at its finest!) on an incredibly bone-chilling day to ask shoppers how they felt about what went down at the meeting.

Here I was, a cub reporter on her first story, and every single shopper I approached turned down my request of a sound bite. What was going on? I tried giving them an extra wide,

10,000-megawatt grin. (That probably scared people even more!) I tried holding out the microphone with the station's logo clearly visible so I looked official. Nothing worked . . . and what should have been a 15-minute assignment turned into an hour. By the time my eyelashes started freezing and I couldn't feel my hands or lips, I was feeling hopeless and re-thinking that abandoned career idea of getting into marketing.

How much longer could I stand doing this? I was not prepared for this weather; I'd wanted to impress my new employer on my first reporting day, so I was wearing a plaid skirt suit—no jacket, no hat, no scarf, no gloves. A middle-aged man in a designer knee-length puffer jacket with fur-trimmed hood walked by, and I yelled out with chattering lips, "Dang, I wish I had what you're wearing!" The man stopped, looked at me with an amused smile, and said, "Hey, didn't your momma tell you to wear some long pants in this weather? What are you doing out in this parking lot in the middle of winter wearing that?!"

Got him. I had inadvertently discovered that by finding common ground and stating the obvious that yes, it was cold outside, opened up the door to conversation. He not only answered my questions, but he became a good source for future stories.

So nowadays when I attend social events, one of the first things I do after putting on my name tag is to get a feel for my surroundings. Is the ballroom ornately decorated to the nines and spectacular? Chances are others will think it's pretty special too, and they won't think it's odd if you make this observation your opening line. Or, what if you and someone both grab for the passed hors d'oeuvres of mini-baby lamb chops with mint jelly that look mouthwatering, take a bite, and realize they're as dry and tasteless as cardboard? You have an instant "in" to comment about how bland the food is to the other person who just shared the same experience. As a mentor once told me, no matter the market or someone's socioeconomic background, race, or religion, it's not hard to find the issues and topics that bind us because we all love, hurt, and feel the same way.

- **Disarm with a Smile:** Like bombs, people sometimes need to be diffused so they don't blow up in your face and turn you down. Many people, even the crabbiest, can be disarmed with a smile. It's that simple. During my first anchoring job in Kansas City, when I thought all TV news anchors were supposed to be stoic, ice-cold creatures if they wanted to appear credible, the general manager told me it was okay to smile. He explained that as long as the story wasn't about death, destruction, or general mayhem, I shouldn't be afraid of showing my personality, and by doing so, my new audience could feel comfortable with me. The same goes with people in real life. A smile is a gesture of kindness, goodwill, and friendliness, and you'll be amazed by how much easier it is to break down someone's defenses when you appear sincerely receptive to an interaction.

- **The Compliment:** A compliment can also be used to disarm someone and get the "in." But please remember that sincerity is key. Compliments are supereffective and they make the receiver feel good. But they must be genuine. People can spot a phony compliment from a mile away. (Think: Paparazzi yelling out compliments to A-list celebs on the red carpet, trying to get them to answer questions.) The automatic answer to, "I love your shoes" or any kind of compliment, is usually "Thank you." Take that thank you and run with it!

One and Done: Don't Go Overboard with Compliments

I once worked with a young cub reporter who was well-liked and worked hard. It also didn't hurt that women (and some men) had a crush on him for his charming good looks and unnaturally thick auburn hair and dimples. His upbeat demeanor was, to me and to my seasoned coanchor, a little . . . phony. Every single day for a week, with a little too much enthusiasm, he would bound into the newsroom and compliment me on my dress:

- Day 1: "Wow, Dion, that color is spectacular!"

- Day 2: "Dion, is that dress periwinkle? It's great for your skin tone!" (Umm, let's just call it blue.)

- Day 3: "Loving the lace, Lim!"

- Day 4: "Really, you've got the best clothes in this place!"

By Day 5, I had had enough of his syrupy-sweet compliments that were obviously half-sincere. There was no way a man needed to compliment a woman's outfit every single day. I exclaimed flat out, "Ricky, I appreciate it, but you don't have to compliment my outfits all the time!" He crept away like a sad puppy with his tail between his legs, and I felt kind of bad.

Later on, I learned from colleagues that Ricky was, with a genuine heart, trying to make conversation and get to know me and wanted me to like him. But the incessant complimenting was just overkill. We ended up with a mutual respect for each other, but not after some rebuilding of trust.

The most effective compliment is one that is offered up right away, that isn't forced and creates a conversation. It's one thing when you tell a baker you love her muffins; that's all fine and dandy. You may get a "Thank you" in return. But what happens when you say, "I love your black sesame muffins so much that I once bought half a dozen for my family . . . and ate them all myself!"? The statement is so different from the same old "love your muffins" that it'll most likely elicit a response that can be turned into a conversation. A compliment coupled with a question works just as well. "Hey, nice work on the monthly newsletter . . . how long did that take you?" Chances are, you'll get a response to a pointed question, too.

STAY MEMORABLE

I always, always, always suggest that my fellow journalist friends attend the National Association of Black Journalists (NABJ) national convention, held once a year in a different city. They usually respond with, "But I'm not black!" This is exactly my point. What's a better conversation starter than, "Yeah, I don't really look like y'all . . ."? Or, six months down the road, imagine running into the head of a major cable network in an elevator somewhere and being able to say, "Hey, weren't you at NABJ, too? I was the lone Hispanic/Asian/Caucasian woman there!"

This tactic can work no matter what field you're in because race doesn't have to be the differentiator. You can stand out in a number of other ways, and not always visually.

One of my favorite examples of being memorable working to my advantage was the night I shared the stage with news legend Dan Rather. We were hosting a panel on the role journalists played in the tumultuous 2016 presidential election, and there were hundreds of foreign students and dignitaries from the United Nations who had been flown in from Washington, DC.

As excited as I was for this opportunity, I couldn't help but think how ridiculous I looked on that night. My foot was swollen to the size of a party balloon, red and itchy after getting stung by a stingray earlier in the month. (If you ever find yourself wading into the Florida gulf between the months of May and October, do the "stingray shuffle" to avoid this same painful fate.) Since the last thing I wanted to do was wheel myself up to the stage in a wheelchair, I had borrowed my senior neighbor's orthopedic cane to use for the night.

So, there I was, hobbling around the ballroom with one of my news idols, wearing a red Tadashi Shoji cocktail dress accessorized with a silver cane. It was pretty hilarious, and Dan and I had a couple of laughs about it. But it did teach me some valuable lessons about the importance of being memorable, including how it doesn't need to be visual, over-the-top, or obvious but it's about letting the real you shine so you're unforgettable when it counts.

- **Nonvisual Memory Making:** When I want to make an impact I always give a "one-notch under freakishly hard" handshake. (Exception: Do not attempt this with children or the feeble. Please don't ask why I know this . . . let's just say I know from an unfortunate personal experience with a terrified child and her grandma.) People seem not to expect a small-framed woman to have such a strong grip. About half the time, the person on the receiving end reacts with a, "Wow, good handshake" and a smile. My response is, "That's what Momma taught me!" When you encounter this person again, they almost always say, "You're the petite woman with a mega handshake!"

- **The Quirks Work:** In any given week I can meet hundreds of viewers, either on a story assignment or at a speaking event. Just between us, when I run into that someone a second time, I have the worst time trying to remember where I met the person or what organization/company the person belongs to—unless there's something quirky about the person. If someone has an odd name (My name doppelganger Dion Lim is the CEO of a tech company . . . *that* is freaky!) or a particularly high-pitched laugh? They're unforgettable. Those mannerisms or unique traits of yours will automatically be associated with that first meeting. Not only will others keep you at the top of mind upon the second meeting, they'll also remember you for the important times, like if they're ever hiring. Even if you don't make grand, sweeping gestures with your arms when you speak or don a signature sky-high top-knot hairstyle, you can achieve standout status by telling a brief impactful story upon first encounter. Maybe it's telling the COO of a hospital how three generations of your family were all born at their campus or revealing that you have to leave the event early because it's your grandma's 100th birthday party the next morning. When you see this person again, or follow up via email, sliding in that little tidbit story will help jog his or her memory.

UH-HUH. RIGHT. YEP. SURE. THANKS. MMHMM (LOOK INTERESTED . . . AND ABSORB)

Just like being a reporter, socializing includes talking to a lot of people. This includes the people who, once you get them going, can talk your ear off. While you may not care about this person's brilliant childhood guinea pig named Rex, or the history of how the United States made a subsonic, jet-powered strategic long-range jet also known as the B-2 bomber (both true stories, the first from a high-ranking politician and the second from a fellow journalist who had been in the TV business for longer than I'd been alive), these ramblers can often be important contacts, or people you need to meet and build a relationship with for your career.

But how do you keep yourself engaged and interested when all you want to do is zone out or fall asleep?

During my time at Emerson College, I would go to parties, and while my friends and I were all semi-inebriated, they'd ask me to do my "reporter face." (The "reporter voice" came later when we were really overserved.) My brow would furrow; my lips would purse into two straight, hard lines; and I would lean in, nod, and murmur, "Mmhmm . . . mmhmmm," and add the occasional, "Yes, oh yes, wow!" for extra comedic effect. It was a party hit, with my peers doubling over in fits of laughter at how ridiculous this parody of a TV news reporter was.

But it didn't work so well when applied to real life.

During my first few years out in the field, I realized that looking interested wasn't enough. When I encountered either a boring interview or the kind where asking one question would open the verbal floodgates, I had all the visual signs of listening mastered, but my brain was somewhere else. This came back to bite me in the butt later. I would have no idea what the person just said, I wouldn't have a good follow-up question, and it would take me longer to put together the story afterward, all because I hadn't actually absorbed anything the person was telling me.

The same concept applies when you run into a Chatty Cathy at work or a social event. The information may be presented in the most boring, convoluted way, but ultimately you still need to retain the basics of what was said. But how do you do that when you're bored to tears?

Listen and Engage with Empathy

As adults, my brother Scott and I always joke about how our father never really fully listened to us. How, when I was in tears over breaking up with my high-school boyfriend, he awkwardly stayed reclined in his knockoff La-Z-Boy and made "Uh-huh" noises and read the newspaper while I bawled my eyes out. I remember getting a feeble and robotic sounding, "It will all be okay" reassurance, and then he was on to the next section of the paper. At the time, not listening when your child is hurting seemed to me to be the most hurtful thing a parent could do.

When my brother was going through hard times with his job and called our dad to let off some steam and seek a comforting ear, all Scott would get were the same murmurs and prolonged periods of silence. (Change the topic to car repair? You couldn't get Dad to shut up!)

In hindsight, I now know my dad does care about us a lot. He just isn't good at talking about emotional things. (Google "Asian parents say I love you." There's a reason why you'll get a ton of parody videos on YouTube and articles on the matter.) Dad was so engrossed in his career and academics because he wanted to succeed and provide a good life for us. This was very common for traditional, old-school Chinese parents. But growing up in a household where listening wasn't valued as much as success and hard work has made me empathize with those who want to tell me a story, or ramble on about something I don't necessarily relate to. Listening shows you care about the person, and even if you don't care about what someone is saying, if you care about the individual, it'll make whatever the subject, however mundane, a bit more palatable. Here's how to train yourself to be more than just a good listener on the outside and truly absorb what is being shared with your ears.

Challenge Accepted!

Do you remember "Simon," the popular 1970s and 1980s game? It was a round electronic game with four colored pads that lit up in a certain order and you'd have to repeat the pattern by pressing on the pads. I played my thrift-store Simon so much that the textured pads were smooth in the center from repeated pressing, and the battery panel came loose and needed to be secured with duct tape. My parents were convinced the game would strengthen my memory and help me achieve educational excellence, while I loved it because it was fast-paced and exhilarating to reach a new record-high sequence.

Just like challenging myself to remember the correct order and colors of the game, I sometimes challenge myself to a mental game of "How long can I stand to listen and how many factoids can I remember?" Suddenly, even the dullest subjects (For me, this includes the Civil War.) or subjects about which I have the least knowledge (all things NFL) become a bit more tolerable when there's a challenge involved. The prize? Being able to engage on the subject later, or just having a personal feeling of triumph from withstanding a verbal vortex.

Maintain Eye Contact

The age-old rule of thumb when meeting people for business is to shake hands, use a firm grip, and look the other person straight in the eye. Part of staying engaged with someone is maintaining eye contact. This is networking 101, right? But what happens afterward? Eye contact is fine, and it shows ownership, caring, and directness. But when it comes to the actual conversation, the last thing you want is the other person to be looking behind you, at the ceiling, at her chipping manicure, or anywhere else. That person is not listening and giving his or her full attention. (It drives me nuts, so I'm extra aware of it when I'm on the listening end.)

I once worked with an anchor (let's call him Oliver) who struggled during his career to climb up the work ladder. He had been passed up for promotion after promotion despite being an award-winning storyteller and being well-liked among the team.

But it was after a team-building lunch and later a breaking-news situation that I realized why. Over Indian samosas, lamb curry, and biryani, he kept looking over at the exit sign. The server. The menu. I knew he didn't have attention deficit disorder, so what was his deal? Here I was trying to tell him about my recent trip to India, yet he looked totally uninterested. Frankly, it pissed me off.

The clincher came after a huge storm that flooded city streets and seemed to have displaced an entire neighborhood. We jumped on set, ready to ad-lib breaking news coming in from our news chopper, and I quickly realized his eye-contact problem was something he did on the anchor desk as well. Instead of looking at me or at the viewers (through the camera lens), he would look off into the distance or look through me past my head. While I was looking at him, listening and absorbing what he was informing our viewers, he was looking somewhere else and giving the impression he didn't care about what he was saying.

Being aware of this and how it affects other people is often enough to break the bad habit of visual drifting. To take it a step further, when you're in a group of three or more think of the "triangle-rule," often instilled in news anchors by consultants and talent coaches. On TV the goal isn't to speak *at* the camera. It's to have a three-way conversation with the audience behind the lens. By forcing yourself to periodically look at the person sitting next to you while addressing the camera is a visual cue to the audience that you're including everyone in the discussion. This eventually becomes second nature in my world on TV, and it will in yours, too. In Oliver's case, I'm pretty sure his inability to consistently engage people visually is what prevented him from moving up in his career.

Too much eye contact, though, can make it seem like you're staring, which makes people uncomfortable. (It's why playing the staring game always ends in a fit of giggles.) In the beginning of my career, when I was the one who had to maintain eye contact with an interview subject or during my live shots, a friend in the TV biz told me to fake a "natural" glimpse downward and to the side—just once or twice for a second or two. It gives the impression you're taking a moment to process what was just said, while at the same time prevents the person you're talking to from feeling awkward or strange because someone is staring at them. It's a trick you can use anytime in any setting . . . just don't forget to look back!

Let 'Em Ramble

In some cases, letting someone ramble can actually be beneficial and result in some information you wouldn't know to ask for. Granted, someone with loose lips can go on tangents and talk themselves into oblivion, but you never know what gems may be unearthed just by listening. You can also make someone ramble on purpose.

One of the first things journalists learn in school (or on the job) is to let silence breathe. When you're interviewing someone, and that person stops talking or isn't very chatty, the natural inclination is to fill the silence. But by resisting that urge and let-ting the silence grow, the interview subject starts feeling the need to avoid any awkwardness and starts talking, and that's the infor-mation you need without knowing you needed it.

Not long ago, I got tipped off by a friend in Tampa about a woman in the San Francisco Bay Area who not only helped stop a laptop thief by chasing down the suspect, but it was all caught on camera. The video was super action-packed, like the best block-buster movie. Here was this woman with blonde, curly hair run-ning like lightning to catch a guy who had stolen someone's laptop from a coffee shop. I couldn't wait to do the story.

The moment our pre-interview on the phone started, I real-ized this lady was going to be a talker, and while I didn't have much time on my hands, I didn't interrupt her passionate recollection of the event. As I "uh-huhed" and took rough notes on the back of a grocery store receipt, the woman glossed over something really interesting. "Yeah, the woman who owns the laptop is like a dance captain of this NBA team..."

What?

To her, the fact that the laptop owner had a high-profile, glam-sounding job didn't matter as much as actually getting the laptop back. But from a news standpoint, this was like hitting the jack-pot! It added an extra level of intrigue and excitement I knew our viewers would love. Turns out, my station loved this extra tidbit, too, and had the story run multiple times. The next day, the piece ended up getting picked up in more than a dozen cities around the country and even went global, with publications in England and Australia reporting the story.

IT'S OKAY TO BE A SEMI-STALKER
(BECAUSE, NEWS FLASH: WE ALL DO IT!)

Every time my contract with a TV station draws to a close and I start going on interviews for anchor/reporter roles in larger markets with (hopefully) larger salaries, my agent sends me what seems like a spy's dossier. It's not just a LinkedIn profile listing where the general manager and news director went to school and their career histories. It's filled with personal notes, like what charities the person is involved with or a funny insider story about a botched wedding speech or a list of hobbies he or she enjoys. I usually fortify these tidbits by doing some social media stalking and by making calls to friends in my network who may know the person to some degree and can shed some insight into this person's personality.

While I realize you may not have an agent providing you with a rundown on every person you're about to meet at a networking mixer/gala/social function, and it sounds supercreepy to do these amateur background checks, a little research can give you a leg up when it comes to conversation. It's an instant "in" to say, "Hey, you're a fellow USC grad, aren't you? I'm class of 2005!" instead of asking, "So, where did you go to school?" It's impressive and shows you care.

One afternoon as I was in the pre-newscast zone, buzzing around like a speed-walking senior citizen at the mall to get all the things I needed prepped for the show, I almost bumped into a sharply dressed man who was surrounded by an entourage of other men. Looking up, I chirped the first thing that came to mind: "Oh, it's Bob Woodruff!"—right to the distinguished journalist's face.

Bob was in town with members of his nonprofit to give a talk about the need for veterans to find work after coming home from deployment. He was set to talk about this in a sit-down interview during our 4:00 p.m. newscast. Much to my surprise, Bob looked amused at my blunt statement and said, "So I hear you're the new kid! These other guys better watch their backs!" He had read my bio and learned that I was the newest member of the ABC-7 team. Not only did that impress me, but it impressed my boss. Here was a guy who, before getting hit by an IED while reporting in the Middle East, had been the anchor of ABC's "World News Tonight."

I'll never forget our conversation that day, and I appreciate that he took time out of his busy day to read a little bit about my background. Going the tiny extra mile to know something about someone ahead of time can go a long way in making the other person feel special and get a conversation or relationship off to a great start.

Assess (Yes, I *Am* Judging You)

No matter whom you're about to talk to, learn what kind of person he or she is and size them up. A businessman in a custom-tailored suit that cost more than your Toyota? A senior citizen who just had hip replacement surgery? This initial assessment is something surprisingly few people think about when approaching someone. You wouldn't go up to a high school principal and say, "Yo, what's happening, teach!" You'd be a little more polite. (If the principal was wearing a Tupac T-shirt, maybe it's a different story.) So, take a moment to consider your best and most thoughtful approach to each and every contact.

An extreme example of this would be a sports guy I once worked with who hosted a regular segment during football season with a different retired NFL player each week. The former athlete would join Isaac at a local high school and do a live remote sportscast from the 50-yard line. The kids loved being on TV, and they would bring signs and noisemakers, and cheerleaders would tumble and break out their best chants for the audience at home.

The problem: While Isaac was a nice guy and a hard worker, he was one of the most straight-laced, buttoned-up nerds on the planet. The guy very well could have had a pocket protector in every shirt that matched his vest. Shiny wingtip shoes aside (Remember, he was at Friday night football games, where the preferred footwear was more high-performance cleats than $400 dress shoes.) Isaac had excellent manners and was the equivalent of a southern gentleman. He was the complete opposite of Johnny, the former football player he was interviewing that week, who was known for his hard-partying ways and carefree, loud attitude and an affinity for "yo momma" jokes.

So, imagine our shock and awe when we tossed out to Isaac in the field and he rolled up his sleeves, loosened his bow tie, and started screaming, "YA'LL READY FOR SOME FOOOOOOTT-BAAALL!?"

This was so out of the norm for Isaac that we were all slightly horrified, yet we were so fascinated we couldn't stop watching. This guy, who looked like Professor Poindexter, was doing the two-step and the Cabbage Patch without a rhythmic bone in his body. Johnny obviously was having a good time, too, because he put a hulking arm around Isaac and said, "You a'ight, white man. You a'ight!"

One common interviewing technique is called "mirroring," where you physically and verbally adopt some of the traits of the person you're talking to. It subconsciously gets the interviewee to feel more at ease because people are more likely to trust others who exhibit similar backgrounds and traits as themselves. The Acton School of Business wrote an article for *Forbes* magazine stressing how mirroring isn't about mimicking. Being a copycat is overkill and can have a reverse effect, or appear phony and make others feel more suspect. Mirroring is all about being subtle in adapting language patterns and pacing and rhythm. If a soft-spoken grandma is trying to order breakfast at the restaurant you're working at, I'm willing to bet you're not going to use your booming voice to blast her into another stratosphere as she orders her poached eggs.

While Isaac probably could have done without the chest bump at the end of the segment, it was clear he had assessed Johnny to be the kind of person he could go out on a limb with and let loose. In his case, it made for compelling television and it worked.

ELIMINATE YOUR FEAR:
THEY PICK THEIR NOSES, TOO

When I give talks at elementary schools, the kids always want to know who is the most famous person I've interviewed. Sorry, kiddos, I haven't interviewed the president, Taylor Swift, or Kobe Bryant. The second question is usually, "Do you get intimidated when talking to celebrities?" and my answer is always a resounding, "No!"

Pretty early on in my career I realized that celebrities, prominent people, and "high-powered" executives are just everyday folks with extraordinary jobs and lifestyles. Some are kind and genuine in real life, while others are bigger divas than you could ever imagine. (One TV sitcom starlet I interviewed during a press junket for a now-defunct show made her assistant cry right in front of me for not selecting the right footwear for the interview. You know, since footwear is so visible in a sit-down interview.)

I bring this up because many people say they're intimidated when talking to Very Important People in a mixing/mingling setting like a gala, or when they bump into them in an unexpected situation like a commercial airline flight or a professional sporting event. My advice: Don't forget, even the famous/rich/important/well-known people sometimes eat Cheetos and get acne and when stripped of their cars/titles/fame, they're just like you and me.

During my Florida years, my coanchor and I hosted a station-sponsored 5K race for cancer research each summer. We were always positioned, air horn cans in hand, on a platform at the beginning of the race, with various high-profile community members. These were usually the mayor and other local politicians, and CEOs of large companies who had made substantial donations to the cause.

One year I forgot my selfie-stick and tripod, so I couldn't do a Facebook Live, as I had hoped. No one from my station was available to help shoot my video—they were all either running the race or giving high-fives to participants and taking photos. So, I looked around my crowded little platform and found an athletic-looking man who was not doing anything particularly important. Since he was just waiting for the race to begin, I gave him a little nudge and handed him my iPhone, and asked if he could record my Facebook video. He graciously agreed and proceeded to record me for about 10 minutes.

Later that day, a throng of viewers and colleagues messaged me to exclaim, "Do you know who you asked to record your Facebook Live?" (Apparently, I had inadvertently shot some video of him as I handed over the phone.) It was the most popular baseball player on the Tampa Bay Rays (Hint: He recently got traded to the San Francisco Giants) who had, not long before, signed a contract worth $100 million.

I laughed pretty uncontrollably for a solid five minutes. That's when I realized it doesn't matter so much who someone is at their day job. They're just like us, shooting shaky Facebook Live videos on a Saturday morning (you know, just with a 94-mile-an-hour fastball). So, the next time you get butterflies in your stomach or are hesitant to approach or network out of your league, remember this story and how at the end of the day everyone is really in the same league.

ESCAPE! HOW TO GRACEFULLY GET THE HECK OUTTA THERE AND LEAVE 'EM WANTING MORE

Sometimes you just need to abort the mission, whether that's because it's almost midnight and you have to get up early to pick up the car from the shop before taking your son to school, or because you've done everything you can to glean what is useful from the event and it's just run its course. How do you extract yourself gracefully from a group of chatty people without appearing rude, or an event where lots of people will notice you're gone? What if it's only 7:00 p.m., and there's still three more hours to go?

Poof! Into Thin Air: Black Houdini

A former coanchor and I joked about his nickname, Black Houdini, whenever he and I appeared at events together. He just had this ability to extricate himself so smoothly from social situations that he'd be gone before you knew it, but it didn't feel bad like he was skipping out. He knew how to have a good time, throw dinner parties, and show up for a drink after work. But he was also tough as nails from years of being a cop in Miami during the Pablo Escobar "cocaine cowboy" days. It was this mix of bad-boy charm and no-nonsense attitude that allowed Reggie (my black Houdini coanchor) to get through any social situation, be adored by the crowd, and make a clean exit, while I ended up having to spend five hours at the same event with no hope for an early escape. It drove me crazy, until I learned how to do it myself:

- **Your Time Is Precious:** Reggie taught me that nobody will care about your precious time like you do. But showing up and giving what little time you do have will leave a lasting impression. Kind of like when you're a kid and the Harlem Globetrotters came to spin basketballs in gym class. You'll never forget the experience, even if it lasted just 20 minutes.

- **Rip Off the Band-Aid:** It's all about making a quick, painless exit, and to do so, you can't engage in any way. The last thing you want is to be stuck there longer and sucked into a new conversation that eats away at your precious time.

- **Good Excuse:** Children, a migraine, your dog needing to pee. All are excellent reasons to slip out of an event. Whichever one you choose, just please make sure it's true.

- **Apologize with Follow-Up:** A quick sorry and promise to "I'll see you at the next one" or "Let's grab coffee" can be enough to appease anyone if they wanted you to stay. By offering a follow-up, it reinforces the notion you do care enough to meet up again in the future.

BRB (Soften the Blow)

There's no way of getting around this one. Sometimes, when you're stuck in a group of people talking and you see someone important to you from across the room, you have to learn to put yourself first and make a clean break. For a long time, I was afraid of hurting other people's feelings by making an abrupt getaway. But like Reggie taught me, being a little selfish with your time and handling the exit correctly can make all the difference.

It was the wedding of the century. Or, at least in my circle of friends it was. My husband and I were at the Vizcaya mansion in Miami where 250 of our closest friends were celebrating the nuptials of our friends Josh and Sari. A marching band was flown in from Barbados to perform. A private fireworks show at the reception required special permitting from the city. And every mover-and-shaker in South Florida was in attendance. The place smelled of opulence and money.

I was still using a fashionable gray-tone orthopedic cane thanks to my stingray encounter three weeks earlier while swimming in Tampa Bay. (It's been said a stingray sting hurts more than giving birth.) So here I was, hobbling along in an elaborately embroidered gown without a care in the world when a gaggle of senior citizens came up to me with mischievous looks on their faces.

"Young lady, you look like us!"

The throng of sassy seniors held up their own orthopedic canes like trophies and began pumping them up and down in the air. This was hilarious. I had been initiated into the Golden Girls club, and I absolutely adored each and every one of these silver-haired soon-to-be centenarians. We hit the dance floor en masse.

Then, after our third song and in mid-boogie, I caught a glimpse of him from across the room. A man described to me as one of the top three wealthiest men in all of Florida for his real estate empire and tech deals. Usually this would not impress me, and it wasn't so much that I was impressed, but more that I was nominated as Champion of the Year for a nonprofit called Best Buddies, and knew he would be my biggest donor if I could just get 30 seconds with him to give my elevator pitch.

As much as I didn't want to hurt the feelings of my new senior besties, I had to break away. I leaned in on my cane and shouted over the music, "Friends, forgive me, but I see a really big fish over there, and I gotta get fed! Will you excuse me for a moment? I'll be right back!" They all nodded and encouraged me to go do my thing.

I successfully scored a $1,000 from Mr. Moneybags. (Pennies to his portfolio . . . but who was I to complain? I was some stranger with a gown and walking stick . . . I'll take the cash!) I later returned to my elderly posse and enjoyed high-fives all around. Here are my tips for successfully breaking away when you feel stuck:

- **Promise to Come Back:** No matter the excuse, telling someone you'll be back always softens the blow of being abandoned. People who are at weddings or in social situations know there are lots of people to talk to, and they understand you sometimes have to go. This can be done with humor ("I must be getting old, it's past my bedtime! I'll drink an espresso before the gala next year!") or with the honest truth.

- **Reach Out After the Event:** If you aren't able to come back (trying to find that person at a big event is like searching for a needle in a haystack), you can always follow-up with the person via email the day after. Or the next time you see the individual, you can lead with a, "Hey, sorry I didn't get a chance to say good-bye the other night . . . it was a zoo in there!" The point (again) is to let people know you care enough to make the effort.

HEY! OVER HERE! CAN YOU HEAR ME!? (GET ANYBODY AND EVERYBODY TO LISTEN)

Remember that feeling in college when your professor droned on in that monotone "Ben Stein in Ferris Bueller" way that put you to sleep faster than an Ambien? ("Anyone? Anyone?") Or how about when you ask the first chair of a big case at your law firm a simple question about where the client files are, but she won't stop talking about her son's new adopted baby from Somalia? You could be the most brilliant mathematical mind, a seasoned geologist who discovered semiprecious rocks in the depths of Kathmandu, or a distant relative of Albert Einstein but it doesn't matter if you can't keep someone's attention.

There's a reason in TV the average local news story is only 20 seconds. Given that the average human attention span is, according to a study by Microsoft, a whopping eight seconds, you don't have a lot of time to capture someone's attention. Once you have that, the challenges don't stop there. It's about keeping your audience focused on what you're saying so they're not checking their Twitter feed, losing eye contact, and totally tuning out what you're saying.

Condition Yourself to Be Aware

The way I learned to be aware of others "zoning out" began with my dad's sinus problem.

During high-barometric pressure or high-pollen-count days, my dad would engage in the "nose waltz." He'd position his index finger horizontally below his nostrils and make a sawing motion; then he'd place the same finger directly in front of his nose and push upward. Visualize a pig's snout. That was my dad.

It was during the nostril pushing that I subconsciously knew my father was in "the zone" and could not be distracted. My mother could be telling him she had an STD and he'd halfheartedly nod, murmur, "Uh-huh, uh-huh. Okay, okay..." and continue watching the Celtics game with one finger pushing his nostrils high in the air like he just don't care. An accomplished chemist who invented all kinds of adhesives and was brilliant with numbers, figures, and chemical equations, listening skills were not my father's forte. Coupled with the cultural divide experienced by a lot of second-generation kids, communication wasn't his strong suit; nor was it ours.

This resulted in my brother and I being hyperaware of our "listening window." If I had a story to tell my dad, or something important that happened at school, it would have to be before those two nostrils were thrust toward the ceiling. This meant not only getting to the point quickly, but telling him what I needed to convey in an attention-grabbing way so he wouldn't lose interest and start tinkering with making a reception-boosting TV antenna out of aluminum foil.

Looking back, this was an excellent training ground to do two things: it made me aware of when the audience was losing interest and what it took to get back their attention and keep it.

When I began my college career and interning at television stations logging tape or fetching coffee, I realized keeping someone's attention would mean I'd get my questions answered more quickly and thoroughly. I also learned that people would take more interest in my projects and I'd get a leg up, compared to the other interns who were less socially tuned in with the people around them. Seemingly important people who actually got paid to work would stop and talk to me in the hallways or at the water-cooler. Below are my tried and true techniques I discovered as a child, honed in my internships, and mastered and put into regular rotation as a reporter and anchor that have become second nature.

Life's a Pitch: Hook Them In and Keep 'Em

Tabloids do it the best. "Bat Boy Spotted at Dairy Queen!" "The President of the United State Is Actually an Alien!" Sleazy, not-quite-true glossy entertainment magazines do too. The producers and writers on one of my favorite guilty pleasure entertainment news programs on TV are virtuosos at the three-word tease: short tidbits that aren't necessarily scandalous or dramatic, but get you to watch through three minutes of commercials. All they need to say is, "Selena Gomez on a Trampoline!" and it seems everyone in the room will turn and pay attention.

Your workplace is not an entertainment show where you need eyeballs to stay glued to a screen so you can collect your advertising revenue. But in many ways, you can use the same strategy to get anybody to pay attention.

- **Make Your First Words a Headline:** Hook in your audience with a bold statement—one you make definitively and with conviction. What's more attention-grabbing: "I'd like to see if we can get some new computers for everybody" or "What's slower than *mo*-lasses? Our company computers!"? This is one time in your day where you can be a little outrageous or out of character to get the eyeballs to glue on you.

- **Get to the Point!** Nothing loses an audience like rambling sentences and scrolling through your camera roll to find the photo you wanted to show everyone. Know your stuff so there's no extra "uhms" that waste precious attention time.

- **Work the Room with Your Eyes:** Your goal should be to make eye contact with every person in the room. It automatically makes you more engaging, plus it's harder for someone to look away and be disinterested if they know you're going to look them straight in the eye to make sure they're alert and absorbing what you say.

MUMBLEMOUTH PREVENTION: PUBLIC SPEAK AND AD-LIB YOURSELF INTO AND OUT OF ANYTHING

Do you freeze when you have to make off-the-cuff remarks? Or when you're asked to give your opinion on something you don't know much about? For an anchor and reporter, breaking news happens constantly, and almost always there is very little information to talk about. You quickly learn to be adept in the fine art of ad-libbing. The good news is you can be good at this with minimal preparation and practice. It's all about conveying the point clearly and precisely with what you've got.

No matter what your career field, this technique comes in especially handy during interviews when unexpected questions pop up. Or those times when your team leader comes down with a case of food poisoning right before he's supposed to give a presentation on behalf of the group and the boss hands it to you. Or perhaps my favorites: when a sweet little grandma who does not give a flying you-know-what asks you about your sex life, or a third-grader asks you how much money you make. Knowing how to jump in and confidently lead communication—even on the fly—will help you avoid shrinking back and panicking.

An End, a Beginning, and the Middle Is All Gravy

The magic to ad-libbing is this: Take a moment, whether it's a split second or a few minutes, to plan out how you're going to start and end your ad-lib. A strong start commands your audience's attention (giving you and your audience confidence you know what you're talking about) and knowing what you'll say to wrap it up prevents the dreaded rambling on at the end. The middle part is the easy part.

I had to think fast the day I heard, "Dion, everyone else's live signal is shot. The lightning wiped out everything, even the anchors on the convention floor. We're coming to you in 10 seconds, stand by."

There was no time to even think, let alone breathe. It was the summer of 2012, and my station was in the middle of extended coverage for the Democratic National Convention, which was taking place in Charlotte, North Carolina, where I was anchoring at the time. Politicians, fellow journalists, and practically the entire globe descended on our usually uneventful mid-sized southern city for a huge week of news. Everyone was working around the clock—running on adrenaline, filing stories, broadcasting live from the convention floor, on riot-watch in the crowded streets, and attending DNC watch parties throughout Uptown. The Queen City was on a national stage, and I knew there would be people from all over the world watching, so this was not a time to be nervous.

There was no time to plan out a script of what to say. Before I knew it, my field producer was shoving a microphone in my hand

and the red light on my photographer's camera was blinking. It was Go time.

All the stars aligned at that moment. Words came out of my mouth . . . and hallelujah! They made sense! Despite not having anything prepared, it was as if my lips were working perfectly in sync with my brain. Colorful descriptions of the rain-soaked roads and the throngs of MSNBC crew members who flooded the outdoor courtyard where I was standing. I recalled things I figured most viewers wouldn't hear about and would be interested in. Encounters with Arianna Huffington, who was holding an event at an aerial yoga studio, and the President Obama dolls for sale that didn't resemble #44 at all. Before I knew it, four minutes of pure ad-lib was over, and I found myself signing off with, "Live at the Epicenter in Uptown, I'm Dion Lim, NBC Charlotte."

Later, those clips were the ones I used on my demo tape to secure a new job in a larger market.

Ditch the Script

A Gallup poll from 2011 cites 40 percent of people are afraid of speaking in front of others. This is second only to a fear of snakes. We're not even talking about the crowds of 500 at career forums, or the thousand-strong crowd of teenagers at a leadership convention, or the 3,000-strong audience of runners about to partake in a 5K. This fear usually spawns even in small settings, like the daily morning meeting or the team-building gathering featuring a group of your peers.

During breaking news situations, I almost always tell my producer to take out any scripts from the prompter. During emcee events, unless the organizer has a lawyered-up script I must read word-for-word, I go without one.

Before you think I must be crazy, let me explain why I do this. People don't like to be read to and when you start memorizing words or phrases, you spend so much time trying to remember the exact word or phrase that you forget the meaning of what you're saying. It'll throw you off balance, so you can't properly convey the rest of what you're saying.

It's also why anchors tweak newscast reads so the scripts are in their own words. For example, instead of "discard," I use the word "ditch"; I also leave room for natural reactions to video. When I'm watching an entire stadium get demolished, I'll allow for a beat to give a genuine "Whoa," because that's the natural reaction to seeing hundreds of tons of steel and concrete crumble in an instant.

- **Rehearse *Just* Enough:** I'm going to be bold here and say it's almost better to under-practice rather than over-rehearse. Here's why: when you practice your speech or presentation too much, you start memorizing words and phrases which can sound staged and disingenuous.

Forgiveness Through Full Disclosure

Whether I'm ad-libbing on set, on stage for an audience of 600, or in everyday life trying to get into a crime scene cordoned off by police tape, a little asking for forgiveness works wonders. They're words to get the audience to understand you're not perfect: To get the police chief to understand you're doing the best you can and you need help; you're up the creek without a paddle, and you're just going to speak from the heart. If an audience knows where you're coming from, they'll be more forgiving than if you force a situation to be better than you're prepared for.

On occasion, I anchor with a sports guy named Larry. Please don't tell him I feel this way (He'll gloat about it for the next 50 years!), but I find him fun-loving, lighthearted, and to be one of the most talented ad-libbers I've ever met. Larry told me he spent years at ESPN where there was often no script and the show was entirely made up on the fly. To me, this sounded slightly horrifying yet exhilarating—a chance to be candid and open with the audience. So, when he made the transition to news and had to read exact copy with names he wasn't familiar with, if he flubbed he would say, "Wow, excuse me, my brain isn't connecting with my mouth right now . . . apologies for mispronouncing that," or "Let me try that again," and then fix his faux pas. By addressing the misstep, he brought attention to his oopsies but also made the mistake blend into his message and delivery, so it didn't seem so out of place.

Surround Yourself with Details

When you're in doubt about what to say in the moment, describe what's around you and the situation at hand in the greatest detail possible. That's been my go-to technique during breaking news and whenever I don't have the answer for something. It's a method that comes in really handy no matter the situation or your occupation. It also gets your audience to pay attention and engage with what you have to say.

For example, you arrive at a four-alarm fire, and 30 seconds later you're live on the air, but you've got no actual facts because you haven't had any time to gather them and the fire chief is busy tending to the emergency. What do you do? Describe what you see. The thick dark smoke billowing from rooftops. The smell of burning debris. The irritating feel of ash blowing in the wind and sticking to your face and eyelashes. It's those details that make a story come alive. Whether there are tens of thousands of viewers at home in their living room, or you're at a board meeting or in front of guests at the company picnic, the surroundings and little details are what transport your audience to another place. This is a great technique to remember if you forget your speech notes at home, or if they accidently blow away in the wind, or there's an equipment malfunction when you're giving a visual presentation. Even if you suddenly have a brain fart in the middle of a presentation to your boss, take a moment to interject some simple and obvious details about the topic; this can act as a stalling technique until you can refocus and get back on track.

When the active shooter situation unfolded at YouTube's headquarters in the spring of 2018, my camera guy and I were the first local news people to arrive on the scene—which was sheer chaos. Police cruisers and emergency responders from every agency under the sun descended on the campus just south of San Francisco. Hundreds of employees were walking out of the building with their hands over their heads. It was a madhouse of live, continuous coverage in a 16-hour day.

There was no time to feel anxiety, to feel the blood pumping in my chest. I didn't think; I reacted, and the words flowed like water because there was so much going on.

When I interviewed an alleged YouTube employee who described the shooter as a man dressed in gray, the anchor back at the station asked me live, on TV, why my interview subject's description went against the police description of the suspect being female. I had no clue why the guy had told me he thought the suspect was a man. But instead of panicking, I instantly responded by explaining some of the details around me. It was a chaotic scene outside the YouTube building, with first responders and the FBI SWAT team swarming the campus.

If it were this hectic outside, I could only imagine the sheer terror and adrenaline someone must have felt being inside the building. That, then, jogged my memory of what a former cop told me about times of high stress affecting physical ability. (It's why snipers practice tactical breathing to keep their bodies calm so their minds are clear.) So that's what I relayed to the anchor back at the station and the anchor moved on to the next reporter live shot.

On day two of covering the shooting, things had calmed down significantly, but the amount of information that could be reported was slim. Not only were police barricades blocking us from getting too close to campus, but Google and YouTube security guards patrolled up and down the street, so no media could ask questions of employees. The programmers, developers, and engineers themselves, 20- to 30-something-year-old techies who distrusted the mainstream media, were quick to shut us down if we even got too close. (No, guy in dark hoodie, skinny jeans, with headphones and MacBook: I am not the "fake news.")

We had no information and a building surrounded by yellow crime scene tape. How was I supposed to go live at four, five, and six o'clock with no sound and nothing exciting to show? By working what we had, that's how. My goal is always to make the scene come alive so the viewer feels like he or she is there in person. Once I started reporting about the heightened security, how the police barricades kept us at an arm's distance, I continued filling in the pieces. I could talk about the tight-lipped employees. They may not have talked, but they had serious looks on their faces as they clutched their laptops to their chests. Where were they walking? To retrieve their personal belongings from their offices-turned-crime scene?

No matter what situation you find yourself in, take a deep breath and realize you have the tools you need to get through it. Everyone loves a good story, and if you learn to observe and describe things in an interesting way, your audience will hang on your every word.

HANDLING PUBLIC SPEAKING SCREWUPS: CUP OF *WHAT*?!

One of the top five questions I get from viewers or from people who learn I'm a TV news anchor is: "How do you not get nervous while public speaking?"

My all-time favorite Larry moment, which ended up being my all-time favorite learning moment, was a doozy. My very first week on the job I was engrossed with getting adjusted to the unfamiliar computer setups, remembering my passwords, and feeling comfortable with my new surroundings. The learning curve was already a bit stressful so trying to appear calm, knowledgeable, and confident for a brand-new audience, who was undoubtedly judging every single thing I did, had me preoccupied and trying extra hard to focus on reading the best I could.

During one particular 4 p.m. newscast, Larry and I came across a story about ice. I don't know what kind of ice. It may have been in relation to a skating rink, cubes in a glass, or Ice Breakers gum. But as I was focusing on not screwing up, Larry's turn to read came up and something ridiculous came out of his mouth. Instead of saying a "cup of ice," he blurted out "cup of ass" to tens of thousands of people.

My mouth instantly went agape. Tears welled in my eyes from the hilarity of it all and my body vibrated from the laughter I tried my best to suppress . . . and then let out in a tidal wave of hysteria. Looking over to the man sitting beside me, Larry had the biggest grin on his face, while cupping his face in his hands. Remember, we were still on live television.

Larry somehow made a moment that would mortify and horrify most people, into something endearing and fun. He and I joked about Freudian slips, becoming a viral YouTube sensation for all the wrong reasons, and his moment of self-deprecation. It made me forget about being perfect, which computer commands to use, and most importantly, the judging audience. He knew everyone would forgive his mistake and find it human.

While this kind of save isn't appropriate for all instances, the audience has the expectation that if you're making something up on the spot, you're not going to have a perfectly polished presentation, but instead, something genuine and real. You'll be viewed as a warm human being instead of a cold robot if you simply show that vulnerable side of yourself.

Address the Fumble Head-On

You'd be surprised at how forgiving an audience can be. Instead of sweeping a mistake under the rug, why not turn it into a relatable moment? During the 2019 Oscars, I was live along the red carpet when a throng of workers started rolling up the protective plastic covering I was standing on. Had I not jumped out of the way, I would have gotten rolled into the carpet! So instead of trying to conceal this unexpected hiccup, I told the audience exactly what was happening: that we were so in-the-moment of Oscars preparations we found ourselves smack-dab in the middle! People loved it and later commented on social media how impressed they were at my ability to tap-dance around this unforseen roadblock. They commented that it felt real and in-the-moment and unlike any-thing they had seen before. Plus, instead of trying to mask a fum-ble, by addressing it head-on, it allows you to clear your brain and do your best work going forward so you're not constantly worried if you masked the mistake well enough.

Just Keep Going

A network reporter posted a terrific throwback video on Instagram of him at his first station trying to do a piece about students who were robbed at a nearby college. For some reason, he said the stu-dents had been gunned down instead of robbed, and just couldn't find the focus to recover. What came out of his mouth was an in-comprehensible jumble of words. His stuttering continued for a good 10 seconds until he figured out his words, and I cringed for him just watching it. Imagine the mortification to make such a sig-nificant and serious flub on live television for the masses! But as a mentor once told me when I had a similar experience, the best thing you can do to quell the anxiety and brain-farting is to take a pause. Even if it's just for half a beat—time enough to get your brain and mouth to reset. Whether you want to apologize or acknowledge the lapse in memory/judgment/speech is up to you. Then, as if nothing happened, keep going. Chances are if you nail the rest of what you're about to say, whoever is listening won't even remember your flub.

BLESS YOUR HEART! (SAYINGS TO KEEP IN YOUR POCKET FOR A RAINY DAY AND EVERY DAY)

Being the first Asian American woman to be at the helm of a week-day morning newscast in Kansas City, then in the main position in Charlotte and Tampa Bay (with a black man at that—double OMG) came with its pros and cons. The research department always leaked to me how my recognition score would be exceptionally high for someone who hadn't been in the market long. To put it bluntly: I didn't look like everyone else, therefore people knew me as "that Asian news lady." It was extremely beneficial for my brand and job security to be known in the community and I was proud to pave the way for other Asian American women and men to enter the market in more primary roles. However, this opened up Pandora's box to a whole host of innocently ignorant questions, like "What kind of Oriental are you?" (Sorry, *Oriental* is for rugs, *Asian* is for people.) or "Is that soup you're drinking chicken noodle?" (No, Vietnamese pho is nothing like the stuff that comes in a red-and-white can.)

So it began. I realized questions and comments like these were becoming frequent, so I mentally catalogued my responses, ready to use them when the situation called for it. The quick responses and quips prevented any possible discomfort from pregnant pauses, uhs, and ums and ensured that the other person wouldn't lose interest as I did mental fumbles finding the right thing to say. (So how exactly *do* you _____?) Being prepared with a quick response also avoided any possibility for the other person to be offended or turned off. It was the verbal upper hand and allowed me to steer the conversation wherever I wanted or needed it to go.

Pretty soon, after becoming adept at responding to these really odd questions about my background (Question: "Are fortune cookies really Chinese?" Me: "I dunno, we ate Pepperidge Farm Milanos growing up!"), I realized the world was full of opportunities to have pre-planned responses to frequently asked questions. The answers would be slightly different each time, but because I had the bulk of the response figured out already, I could focus on the delivery of the response or story and make it *pop*.

The idea of having a pre-canned response works with even the most run-of-the-mill questions like, "Where did you and your husband meet?" (Short answer: On a story about neighborhood debauchery . . . the neighborhood where he lived in college.) These answers become much better when I include certain details that usually are forgotten in a regular recounting of the tale. Turns out the person asking the question was always delighted to hear that my now-husband saw me from his window and started yelling, "Hey, news lady!" and came out and asked to be interviewed. The rest is history.

When you're faced with stickier comments and questions, having ready retort that works can correct the other person without appearing to be a know-it-all. In many instances, this can be done with a bit of humor. When viewers or coworkers—or anyone, come to think of it—ask me about my husband's job and they find out he plays poker professionally, the first question is often, "Really? He can make money doing that?" followed by the comment, "Good thing you work to support his habit!" It used to drive me crazy because people clearly didn't understand what is involved with being a poker pro, and were insinuating he didn't contribute financially to our relationship. My trained response to the first question is, "Trust me. If he didn't, we wouldn't be together!" and to the second is, "Hardly! It's more like the other way around . . . I'm the one with a designer handbag addiction!" Because my response is instant, it is more impactful than stuttering to come up with a logical response, and the humor softly corrects the other person. The same applies in your work setting when you frequently get asked a question that rubs you the wrong way or is an incorrect assumption. A common one I hear from my friends that has also happened to me is that after a promotion someone expects you to have the same duties as your previous job title. When I was bumped up to anchor from being a reporter, viewers and my colleagues would still call me a reporter. It happened so often yet I didn't want to be a snotty ice princess by correcting anyone. Instead, my canned response would be a delayed one addressed later. If the person asked me what my reporting story was, I'd just say, "Oh, I'm in studio anchoring today." and let the other person figure it out. That way, I wouldn't have to address the issue head-on or make any concrete corrections myself. Having a preset response isn't being a robot. It's being smart in addressing potentially sticky, strange situations and lets you move on with your conversation and day.

INSTANT EXPERT

Whatever your field of expertise, you probably get the same questions each time someone learns what you do for a living. Remember, to them you're an expert, so they are excited to learn your answers to their questions. If you're a doctor, be prepared to listen to people's symptoms when you're at a social gathering ("Could you just look at my toe for a minute?"); if you're a teacher, they'll probably comment on "All that time off you get—every holiday and all summer!"; if you're a flight attendant, you're bound to hear, "Don't you get to travel all over the world for free on your days off?" So, turn those sometimes-inappropriate comments and questions into a library of thoughtful, witty, and/or funny responses that you can use anytime, anywhere. Having those answers ready frees you up to focus on steering the conversation in the direction you'd like it to go.

SEAMLESS STEERING

Remember those cheesy 90s sitcoms where the jokes were so dorky and overacted that they were funny, and a laugh track played in the background? When an awkward situation would pop up and the character would do an obvious misdirect and say, "Look over there!" and point to some far-off distance and run away? While you can't be quite that obvious while talking to your supervisor or a client, you can gently steer the conversation to a slightly different yet related topic so as not to make the other person feel like you're purposely trying to snake out of a conversation.

A former producer of mine (let's call him Monty) was a total movie buff who used famous quotes in everyday speech. The man really should have been a film critic! It seemed he could recite lines from any and every movie (those from the gangster genre in particular) from 1940 to the present day. This of course was terribly "inside baseball" for someone who doesn't watch a whole lot of movies (TV shows and YouTube videos are more my jam), and when Monty would stride over to my desk to make small talk, my instinct would tell me to get up and hide. However, this was not a realistic or normal thing to do in the workplace, so as soon as Monty would start reciting lines from *Rambo*, *The Godfather*, or *Pulp Fiction*, I would use what little I knew about those movies and segue to get him to talk about something else . . . like work.

"Hah, what do you think is more difficult, being a mobster or a TV news reporter? After the week we had with that huge rainstorm and team coverage, I vote TV news reporter. How did you think we handled it?"

The Key to Getting This to Work Is Trifold

1. Touch on what you do know about the subject (as little as it may be).

2. Link it in a general way to the topic you do want to talk about as if something about subject A jogged your memory about subject B.

3. Ask a question on your chosen issue. This is imperative because it forces the other person to answer the specific question and propels the conversation forward, not backward into the topic you feel uneducated about.

By mastering this skill, you're not only getting to the root of what needs to be discussed, but you're also saving yourself time and giving off the appearance of entertaining the other person's interests.

While you'll never be able to predict every crazy verbal minefield you're likely to encounter in your work environment, you'll find the anxiety and uneasiness subside the more you deploy these techniques, no matter what situation you find yourself in.

More Than a Pickup Artist
Connect and Keep Up with Anyone and Everyone

*C*ONGRATS! You have survived the real-life social network. But your job is far from over. Now that you're armed with some of my tried-and-true tactics for getting the "in" in any circumstance, you'll want to perfect your techniques for growing your professional circles.

During social events, it's one thing to follow the age-old advice of making sure to have enough business cards handy. But let's be honest. How many of those business cards get inadvertently buried at the bottom of someone's handbag, or end up collecting dust on a desk or getting tossed in the trash? Then everything you've just worked so hard for has just gone down the drain. Here's another secret: The bulk of making contacts and friends and relationships doesn't come from pre-packaged networking events.

It comes from everyday life . . . and those contacts can happen in some of the most unexpected ways.

Today, it's not just about business cards and networking mixers. There are so many more ways to connect with someone, whether it's through social media or while waiting in line to get your oil changed at the body shop. Your network is everywhere.

THE MOST HIDDEN
AND UNLIKELIEST OF GEMS

Just because someone doesn't appear to be "useful" for your career today doesn't mean they won't come in handy sometime later. The architect who helped us remodel our house told us about a client he had who wanted to hire him to help her renovate a small condo. He was hesitant to take on the project since it was only a few hundred square feet and he had some much higher-end projects that would be more lucrative. But since he liked this client, he took on the job. Little did he know that four years later, that same client would reach out and hire him to be part of an $8,000,000 home project! (I wonder what happened in those four years!?)

I can't stress enough how important it is not to take others at face value. Here in San Francisco, the 21-year-old in the beat-up hoodie and holey jeans may have just sold his tech startup for $50 million! The seemingly meek grandma down the street who bakes cookies for you could be best friends with the governor of California! There is even a poster of me on the wall at my station with one of my favorite sayings: "I'm amazed by what can happen when you strike up a conversation. Seemingly ordinary people suddenly become remarkable."

- **How to Identify These People:** Here's the secret to identifying the hidden gems: talking. Not by prying but through regular, everyday conversation. By treating everyone fairly and as your equal and taking just a few minutes out of your day to chat, they'll naturally open up about people they know, those they're related to, and sometimes about more than you'd ever imagine.

- **Equals:** This is probably a good rule of thumb for life in general, but especially applies to the workplace and your career. By treating your intern or the new employee as well as you do your general manager and esteemed president, you're showing him or her a level of respect. That'll come back one day when your former intern becomes your new VP.

THE POWER OF THE ASK: FEAR WHAT?

To our circle of nerdy journalism friends, Archer is known as "The Closer." He may get a lot of criticism for being a little too persistent (even aggressive) when it comes to networking, but nobody can deny how his incessant emailing, direct messaging, and LinkedIn connecting produces some pretty miraculous results.

What he has taught me is that it's all about going one step beyond the initial meeting, first email, or friend request on social media. His two-step method is to be direct (because you'd be surprised at how many people are *not*) and then nurture the relationship.

It was at a journalism convention for Asian Americans that I was able to observe Archer's shameless networking in action.

He strode up to the president of one of the top TV networks in America and introduced himself. Not only did he start chatting him up, but Archer asked for the guy's personal cell phone, later texted him asking for an invitation to the network gala that night, reserved only for—you guessed it—people who worked for the network, which Archer did not belong to. Lo and behold he got invited to the party and spent an evening rubbing elbows with the top network executives and multi-million-dollar anchors.

For a week after Archer's miracle encounter and follow-up with the network president, all my friends and I could talk about was how we could never have the chutzpah to do the same thing. But why not? The worst that could have happened was Archer would get a "no."

Sure, as a reporter I ask for contact information and ask questions to push the envelope all the time. But to ask for the phone number of someone who was the head of an entire TV division, and who had the power to hire and fire anyone, approve multi-million-dollar salaries, and change the course of modern TV media as we knew it just sounded downright scary. Wasn't it? Could there be some truth to a 2018 University of Cambridge study that women are 2.5 times less likely to speak out and ask questions in an academic seminar? If this statistic applies at work, it's high time we change that!

It wasn't until the death of San Francisco's beloved mayor did I fully understand the power of the ask.

How Many Numbers Did You Get?

I was assigned to cover Ed Lee's memorial at the city hall rotunda. It was a grand affair, with fire engines draped in American flags at the entrance and a visitation line that stretched around the block.

Guests included pro athletes like Joe Montana and Barry Bonds, celebrities like hip-hop singer will.i.am, and dignitaries from across the globe. The late mayor of San Francisco was known as an anti-politician, extraordinary because of his ordinary demeanor, bad jokes, and approachable, friendly smile, which made him a lot of friends.

When I came back from the memorial, my coanchor for the evening asked me how many numbers I got. I was perplexed. What did he mean by numbers? Numerology numbers? After reading a story about an 80s rock star getting inducted into the Rock & Roll Hall of Fame, he explained by whipping out his cell phone in the commercial break and slid it across the plexiglass desk to my side.

The message on the screen read: "Hey Man, congrats on the induction . . . just read it on the news. Hope you're well, let's grab dinner the next time you're on tour." I was stunned. How on earth did my coanchor get the personal cell phone number of one of the biggest rock icons of all time?

By asking. Not for the musician's agent, assistant, or manager, but my coanchor said he made a habit of asking for direct cell phone numbers of all the people he interviewed, no matter who they were. He proceeded to scroll through his contacts list to show me everyone from librarians and Judge Judy to former heads of state and the direct line to the makeup artist for "American Idol."

Shortly after, I tried this with a *Time* magazine person of the year, the organizer of the SF Women's March, and the mayor of a nearby city. Not one of them batted an eyelash. Granted, they weren't Beyonce, but these were prominent people who helped me get in the routine of asking, so it now feels like second nature.

- **Purposeful Asking:** My job is the perfect excuse to ask for a phone number. I'll couple the ask with a reason. When I asked for an Olympian's phone number, I did it because I wanted to text her some photos from the event she was hosting. A reason makes it harder to say "no" . . . just make sure it's a legit reason! It helps soften the fear on your end and the other person is more inclined to say "yes" because there's purpose to the ask and he or she knows you're not just getting a phone number for fun.

- **Appropriate Asking:** Setting yourself up for the best possible odds of a "yes" is just as important as having the confidence to make the request. You don't have to be like this anchor and ask for personal cell phone numbers. If a business card with work email is enough for you, then ask for it, develop a relationship, and then go in for the personal mobile number. There's no rule saying you have to ask for the world when just getting a piece of it is enough to get the job done.

- **The Everywhere Ask:** Some of you may feel asking for a phone number at a memorial is not appropriate. In many ways it's not. Would you dare request contact information from someone as weeping family members are on stage? Never! But after the ceremony it would have been perfectly fine to start talking to the woman next to you, realize you've got things in common (perhaps fond memories of the deceased) and want to keep in touch for the purpose of reminiscing. I've asked for business cards at baseball games, the grocery store, and even while traveling overseas on vacation. It may not always be at the top of your mind, but your potential untapped network is all around.

Keep Up with the People You Meet

Okay, you've gotten past asking and got the business card or cell phone number. But what's the use in asking, if you don't either A: reach out and call/text/email, or B: follow through and keep up the relationship? It's like the feeling I get about fellow reporters, anchors, or interns in the TV business I meet through work, but who then drop off the face of the planet only to be heard from again when they want something. I'm less inclined to help someone I think is using me for something.

The problem is, maintaining a contact and turning the two- or three-minute initial connection into a business relationship/ friendship has challenges. Either because you forget to reach out, are afraid of being too forward or annoying, or just don't know how important keeping these relationships is. Sure, I have a stack of business cards at my desk and I get it, there are only so many hours in the day, so writing follow-up emails and making calls isn't always feasible. But I have several tried-and-true ways to keep up that don't take much time and are supremely effective:

- **This Reminds Me:** One foolproof way to keep up a relationship is to drop a quick note when something you see triggers a thought about that person. Several weeks after meeting a bakery owner at a gala and getting her business card (Seriously, she gives the Parisian croissants a run for their money!), I found myself eating a substandard supermarket croissant from a catered lunch and snapped a photo of it, and sent a one-line email to the baker saying, "Wish I was eating one of your flaky pastries, not this boxed lunch junk!" The photo made the correspondence funny and memorable and the email was so casual it wouldn't scare her into thinking I was trying to be too forceful in solidifying our relationship.

- **Social Media Minders:** These days, we have the benefit of social media to help us with keeping up relationships. Sometimes all the posts can feel like too much, like a few radical relatives of mine who like to broadcast their extreme political views multiple times a day on Facebook. But there are so many opportunities to keep up with people you meet via Instagram or other digital groups. Following the person and then tagging him or her, commenting, or giving a simple "like" keeps you in people's general mind space without forcing yourself into the picture. So, when you *do* need something or want to reach out, you'll be in their periphery.

- **The Power of Coffee—Start Small:** For the people I feel more of a connection to and want to really solidify a relationship with, I ask them to join me in a short, efficient, and low-commitment activity like meeting for coffee. If we really hit it off, lunch. Sometimes it's as easy as, "There's something I want to pick your brain about" or proposing a collaboration.

Networking doesn't have to be a series of boring events nobody wants to attend. Instead, remember that the world is your oyster, and everyone in it has a story. By treating people with respect and finding something interesting to connect with them over, you'll build your network without any more effort than you put into ordering your venti caramel frappaccino with extra whipped cream.

THE GIRL FROM REDDING:
HOW TO ASK THE RIGHT WAY

Hate to break it to you, but once you've mastered the practice of asking for a business card, a phone number, or a chat over a matcha latte to build your network, the act of asking gets a whole lot harder from there. There will be times where you'll need to ask your manager or a colleague or client for something you almost definitely think will result in a "no." To make matters worse, you're intimidated because you think if the answer *is* "no," it's a poor reflection on you for even asking. Right? Maybe. There's a method to not only summoning the courage to ask for something you want or need, but to then arm yourself and be so prepared for the ask and any questions that may arise with it that your odds of getting a "yes" increase significantly. One instance of this that stuck out in my mind involved a rookie reporter and a wall of thick smoke and smoldering embers.

Kensie, the Wonder Reporter

Tap, tap. I felt a finger on my shoulder. "May I ask you a question? You're so much more experienced than I, and I don't know what to do."

I turned around and saw a young woman with windswept hair, dirt-smeared jeans, and a polo, holding a cell phone and a tiny video camera attached to a tripod. Judging by her lineless skin and saucer-sized terrified eyes, I pegged her to be no more than 22 years old, and a rookie reporter in the tiny town of Redding, California.

We were both on assignment, covering the deadly Carr Fire about three hours north of San Francisco. This was one of the worst fires in the state's history, charring more than 200,000 acres and killing six people. A mix of wind, flames, and an exploding gas line took the lives of a great-grandmother and her two great-grandchildren, both under the age of 5. It was a horrific and tragic story and we were less than 100 feet away from the home where it happened.

I recognized the young woman from the group interview moments earlier when a member of the Shasta County Sheriff's office agreed to go on camera. The spokesperson was tight-lipped, as they often are during an active investigation. We were fed a bunch of canned-sounding, politically correct responses that didn't really say much. But after some careful prying (ahem, by yours truly), I managed to get the deputy to tell the group his team was searching for "bone fragments."

On the inside, I dropped the mic. Those two words were the most attention-grabbing (yet most explicit and chilling) part of his interview. The words were shocking and graphic and conveyed the seriousness and deep sorrow of the situation. This was the added detail I needed for my story to be compelling and not like every other competing station's fire story that night.

Back to the young woman, who introduced herself as Kensie, and her question. She was about to go Facebook Live and wanted to know if, by saying the words "bone fragments" on TV, she would come across as insensitive. After telling her to use the words, but attribute them to the deputy, I realized how preposterous her situation was. Here she was, standing at barely five feet tall, juggling all sorts of equipment in a fire zone, trying to figure out how to tell the story and go Facebook Live and Tweet and post to Instagram. It was too much. What, were we going to throw a rabid pack of coyotes at her and see if she can handle fighting them off, too?

Kensie shook her head wistfully as she glanced back at my own photographer and live van. In the same tone as if to say, "It is raining outside," she said her station regularly requested she shoot by herself in dangerous situations. Just the other day she spent almost 18 hours by herself in the field during a police standoff with an armed shooter. Was this a joke? Didn't her station management understand as a single female reporter at night she was a walking target?

I looked Kensie in her big Bambi eyes (that undoubtedly still saw the world in full technicolor splendor) and said as firmly as I could while using all my might not to grab her by the shoulders and shake some sense into her, said, "Kensie. You *must* tell your station you can't be doing this by yourself anymore. A story where you're getting paid $12 an hour isn't worth getting yourself killed over."

Kensie stared back at me blankly and I knew what she was going to do. Nothing. This was her first job, she had only been there a year and was up for an important promotion that would raise her salary by $4 an hour. (Hey, $16 an hour is more than a lot of people right out of school in television news could wish for.)

She would learn eventually to stand up for herself, and in the right way. But I prayed it would be before she got herself injured . . . or killed.

The Kensie incident really got me thinking about the way we as women ask for things.

The way we're doing it (or not doing it) is preventing us from getting what we want. It's sacrificing our morals and beliefs and causing us to sell ourselves short. We're either too scared or don't believe we deserve what we're asking for.

The key to asking for something at work is to actually make your question or request in a way that showcases what you can offer and how the other person and your organization can benefit. A case so strong, there is no choice but for the other person to say "yes," or at least some version of it.

- **Ask by Not Asking at All:** You'd be surprised by how many times asking for something doesn't require a sentence with a question mark at the end. Instead, a statement can often lead to the other person automatically offering an answer. For example, while covering a fire in and around the tight-knit community of Thousand Oaks in Southern California, I had brought my ridiculously oversized station jacket to a press conference with first responders. A photographer from a competing station snapped a photo of me during my live report and, much to my dismay, the jacket looked more like a mumu, billowing almost to my knees, given it was four sizes too big. Not wanting to ask for a smaller jacket since I had already asked for a station umbrella a short time earlier, the next time I saw the person in charge of the company logoed outerwear, I showed her the photo. She was so shocked at how ridiculous the blue tent jacket looked on me she made a beeline to the supply closet and unearthed the last one in my size.

This not-asking-but-asking technique can also work in the form of feedback. After a particularly stressful night covering a voter return party for California's governor, I knew my performance was not the best. An elbow-to-elbow crowded platform of journalists didn't make for the most comfortable conditions to think, and the sheer amount of noise was distracting. Our supposedly noise-cancelling microphone headsets were not as effective as the ones used by other networks. I didn't want my superiors to think I couldn't work well under tough conditions, but I did want the station to consider investing in quality noise-cancelling headsets. So, during our after-assignment debrief, I mentioned the intense decibel level at the beginning of the conversation along with some other points and then sprinkled in the fact other stations had over-the-ear headsets, which made communication between the team and the reporter much easier. There was no question needed as my bosses came to the conclusion themselves.

- **Reinforce the Positive:** My literary agent is the best at giving out feedback because she uses the sandwich technique: praise first, feedback second, more praise to wrap up. It softens a critical message so it's easier to digest. The same applies for setting up an ask. Example: "Your TEDTalk changed my life! I'd love to chat with you more if there's a number where I can reach you. My family found your message so inspiring."

- **Let Others Answer Before You Can Ask:** Sometimes you need or want something, and the answer is so obvious and crystal-clear that asking may not be necessary at all. All you need to do is just give the issue a nudge. For example, after realizing I had 20 days of unused vacation days and just 90 days in which to use it all, I worked in the phrase, "Hopefully I don't burn out—I've got seven public appearances over the course of the next two months!" near my scheduling manager. On her own, she realized I hadn't had a day off in six months and asked me that afternoon what days I'd like and that I'd get first dibs. Too often the questions you need to ask are an oversight to others. They just don't realize they're issues. Instead of having to bring up the issues constantly, steering others to an answer can cast you in a better light and you'll get what you want at the same time.

If I were in Kensie's beaten up sneakers and knew what I knew today, here's how I would have made the hypothetical ask:

- **Positives:** "We had a very productive few days in the fire zone. I'm proud of the producers and team back at the station."

- **Proof of Performance:** "With everyone's help I was able to post two Facebook lives and turn six live stories, which were the top clicked on stories at our station website."

- **The Non-Ask Ask:** "Back-to-back 18-hour days were tough and there were times I thought I'd fall asleep at the wheel or be too exhausted to stay focused and away from the flames."

- **Solution Proposal:** "Next fire of this magnitude, we should double-team. Even if not for the entire shift, but just overlapping some hours. This way, we can be safer and less prone to accidents on the job, and at the same time produce even more content with a second pair of hands and eyes."

Sure beats saying, "Working 36 hours in two days sucked!"

THE ASK: ACTUALLY A SHOWCASE OF *YOU*

Whether it be asking for a raise, a vacation day, or even something trivial like a new pad of neon Post-it Notes, I always think of the ask as an opportunity to showcase how what you're asking for is going to benefit the other party and the greater good. It's not about your wants and needs. It's actually about theirs. The last thing your boss wants to hear is how you want to take, take, take. But asking in a way that reinforces the positive will get you a much higher "yes" rate, all the while making you look good. Even if you don't get an immediate or a vehement "yes," the other person gets to see why you're valuable and worth saying "yes" to when the opportunity arises.

Turn Smelly into a *Win* (Reinforce the Good)

One of the best things about being a reporter is being able to experience events or phenomena you ordinarily wouldn't be a part of. Broadcasting live from the Democratic National Convention arena 15 feet away from Michelle Obama. (Yes, she is as gorgeous and striking in person as on TV.) Getting into the must-see Museum of Ice Cream before the general public. Being on the hardwood at the NBA Finals alongside towering giants, bright lights, and booming music.

One week, what I really wanted was to see and smell the infamous corpse flower. I knew it would be disgusting . . . but in the same sick way we all are fascinated enough to stop and watch a car accident on the highway, I just couldn't resist satisfying the curiosity of experiencing something so nasty and weird.

The *Amorphophallus titanum*, AKA the corpse flower, known as the world's smelliest plant, only grows in the wilds of Sumatra and only blooms every 7 to 10 years. The rarity of this flower, coupled with the sheer intrigue of smelling something so foul it's described as decomposing flesh mixed with bad blue cheese, was too much for me to resist.

When the infamous plant started to bloom at San Francisco's Conservatory of Flowers, I got on it right away, emailing the communications director and reading up all I could in anticipation of the big day. Turns out, nobody at my station was as jazzed as I was about doing the story because it had been done before. (The conservatory had apparently an entire army of corpse flowers ready to go in some back room, so they were never short of blooms.) The plant also wasn't new anymore, so chances are, viewers already knew about it.

The day of the pitch in front of a dozen managers, producers, and peers, I decided to go all-in on a three-step pitch focusing around the things I knew they wanted:

- Digital videos in addition to my TV story, which would be translated into online hits and extra revenue for the station

- Facebook Live with the conservatory's scientist to answer viewer questions and boost engagement, reminding everyone of the high viewership numbers for my previous videos

- Content for the station Instagram account, which I would be in charge of so the rest of the web team could focus on other work

On the inside, this is what I really wanted:

1. Avoid paying the $6 admission fee and battling big crowds on a Saturday morning (Remember, my parents raised me to be "frickin' frugal.")

2. Satisfy my own personal curiosity of what it smelled and looked like

3. Have fun photos for my own Instagram to share the experience with my followers and friends

4. BONUS: Avoid covering a boring court case, being live at the scene of a car crash, or possibly seeing a dead body or shooting

Guess who got to do the story? Not only did the proposal impress my managers, I never once had to use the phrase "Can I" or "I want." When you present something that benefits the other person or your company/organization, it becomes irresistible and greatly increases your chances of getting the "yes." It gives the impression you're a team player, looking out for your colleagues and if you benefit from this, it's just an added bonus.

Talk to the Voices
in Your Head
Communicate with
Yourself First, in
Order to Communicate
with Others

THIS SOUNDS TERRIBLE, but it's true. Early in my life I felt so ugly that all I wished for was to be a white person. Even an ugly white person would do. That would be at least better than being Chinese. Later in my career, despite growing into my flat bridgeless nose, figuring out how to do my cowlick-riddled, genetically faulty hair, and wearing eye makeup to accentuate (and not resemble a raccoon), I still felt like a freak when I hit the air. I was the first Asian American woman to be at the helm of a weekday morning newscast in Kansas City, and the first Asian American to sit in the primary 5/6/11 p.m. newscast time slots in Charlotte and then again in Tampa. (My coanchor in Florida, an African American man, and I used to joke hurricanes would pale in comparison to when viewers saw us together . . . they wouldn't know what hit them!)

Instead of feeling authentic, I focused my efforts on fitting in and putting on a facade. The perfectly coiffed anchor-hair helmet, coordinated J.Crew blazer/pearl necklace/shoes combo (J.Crew is so *not* me, by the way), and the big shiny Crest Whitestrips smile on Facebook. Without it, I was insecure about myself because I was different (for a lot of other reasons, which you'll read about soon), and it showed in the way I performed at my job and interacted with others—especially with those who were insecure in their own ways, too.

This public show, this fake display of what I thought I was supposed to be on TV, wasn't sustainable at all and soon this flawless veneer started to crack. I'd go home, peel off the outfits that felt more like a straightjacket, and surf the web, longing to one day wear bright colors like the women on "Good Morning America." My spirit was broken, and I felt trapped playing this character for most of my day. A blurry waterfall of tears would pour from my eyes frequently as I drove home at the end of my shift because I felt stuck in this artificial TV world I created for myself. There was even a spare pair of prescription glasses in the glovebox for the times my contact lenses fell out from all the crying.

Back then I had no idea how important authenticity was to happiness, which, turns out, directly impacts your success and longevity with your employer. A 2018 study by analytics firm Gallup analyzed why employees leave their jobs. One reason: workers not feeling like they could grow and develop their skills and be appreciated. How can you do any of those things when you're not being the true version of yourself and are instead so worried about what other people think of your performance? Your boss won't be able to see what you're truly capable of unless you're able to communicate with yourself first.

This cycle of being uncomfortable in my own skin had to stop, but I didn't know how to fix it. How could I learn to get along with my colleagues, feel good about my job, and get ahead when all I wanted to do was crawl up in a ball wearing pajamas, watch re-runs of HGTV's "House Hunters," and eat sour cream and onion Pringles by the tube?

Unless you're ready to step back and honestly assess yourself, identify your own vulnerabilities and faults, and face them head-on, you'll never be able to effectively communicate with others. After all, the journey to communicating to the top, begins with learning to communicate with yourself first.

DION LIM IS NOT CONNIE CHUNG: MAKE YOUR OWN NAME (BECAUSE IT'S MORE THAN ENOUGH)

Growing up with my Tiger Mom meant everything was a competition. Which one of my dad's colleagues had the prettiest wife? Who in my fourth-grade math class could recite multiplication tables the quickest? (Mom: "Ay-yah, but Brittney *sooo* dumb!") To be number one was to reign supreme and bring honor to the family. This is totally a cultural thing, and why sociologists determined certain Asian countries like China and Japan have the highest suicide rates. The pressure to be the very best can often take the ultimate toll.

What I've discovered throughout the years is that you don't have to be number one, make the most money, or be the most popular or talented. But if you're comfortable with who you are and you can let others see that, these things will naturally happen. I promise.

When I started my first anchoring job in Kansas City back in 2007, viewers would yell out, "Hey Connie!" or "Hey Newslady!" whenever they saw me in public. Being new they didn't know my name and assumed I was just a generic newsreader, or, since I'm Asian, was akin to the only other Asian American TV news anchor they knew, the legendary Connie Chung.

At first this was pretty amusing. Here I was, in my twenties, being compared to a woman who was, at the time, in her sixties and not even on TV very much any longer. It made for a funny story to tell friends and family and, in a way, it was flattering to be compared to my childhood idol. But deep down, I knew people weren't calling me Connie because I was a legend or as talented as she was, and it started to really bother me. I wanted to scream back, "Actually, my name is Dion! I have my own qualities and talents too!"

Luckily (or maybe I should say, at first, unluckily), the problem eventually solved itself.

Let me explain.

Because I was so inexperienced and young when I started my job, and knew there were so many people who didn't think I deserved to be there, I did what I thought it took to stay alive: copy what everyone else was wearing, how they sounded, and what they looked like. This meant a boxy suit in gray, brown, or black, over a cami in the summer or turtleneck sweater in the winter. Deepening my voice to sound like Walter Cronkite (*so* ridiculous), and copying the sayings and words said by the news anchors around me.

One day, when I was so hyperfocused on making sure the words coming from my mouth sounded authoritative and had just the right cadence, I didn't even realize I had just pronounced the name of then Speaker of the House John Boehner (bay-ner) as John *Boner*! No more than three minutes after I stepped off the anchor set, I got a call from my VP of news, who wanted to have a "talk." Gulp. This was it. I had really messed up and my anchoring days were over before they ever really got started. Instead of reaming me out for the mistake as I had anticipated, he smiled warmly in a gentle grandfatherly way and asked, "Dion, do you know why you're here?" Since there was that lawsuit filed by three older female colleagues, alleging they were passed over for the job I had (you'll read about that in a moment), I murmured, "Because I'm cheap? Because I'm Asian?" Without missing a beat he said, "No, Dion. I hired you because of *you*." He went on to explain how he wanted me to be *me*. To smile, to wear what I usually wore in a professional setting, and most important, to relax. As if a magic spell was cast over me, those words were the first turning point in my career. This was the green light to show the world who I really was and what I could accomplish as me.

That night I went home and put all my ill-fitting suits and turtlenecks into a garbage bag to donate to Goodwill. The next morning, I donned a colorful wrap dress for the first time. It was as if I had found some magical key to the kingdom, because that dress allowed me to move my arms around freely when explaining things. The openness of my body translated into a more conversational tone when reading scripts. As the comfort level increased, I started letting out a laugh during the kicker story at the end of the show. (That's the feel-good story usually about a champion weightlifter senior citizen or the world's largest koala baby.) Instead of being worried about how someone else would cover a story, I infused my own creativity in reporting—like running in heels alongside a man who was trying to run through all 50 states.

Viewers would take notice and start yelling, "Hey Dion!" or "I watch you on Channel 9!"

This was my first experience with the term "branding" before it became a hip buzzword. It got me thinking about what else I could do to use *me* to make a name for myself as Dion Lim. Because, at the end of the day, yes, we're all capable of doing the work. But what sets you apart from the cogs in the wheel is your authentic self and allowing it to shine through.

Make Your Own Name: What Makes You Happy?

This seems like a pretty basic question, but you'd be surprised at how many people don't think about what makes them happy. They also don't see the benefits of what can happen when you discover the answer. For me, I love meeting ordinary people who do extraordinary things. The adrenaline rush of figuring out the puzzle pieces of a story. Being on stage, giving motivational talks to students or professionals, and the satisfaction of knowing that sharing my mistakes, stumbles, and experiences can help others. At one point, I was making upwards of 30-plus appearances at schools and conferences, and giving private studio experiences every year. This made me stand out as someone who wanted to help the community, which then, in turn, provided a lot of opportunities. For example, even though I was newer than most of my counterparts, viewers would tip me off to exclusive stories or invite me to exclusive events because I was so visible in the community. I was able to turn what I loved doing into my brand.

When I ask this question to my friends in other professions, they'll say, "I love knitting, but I can't knit at the hospital! I'm a nurse!" Nobody said you couldn't knit at home or during your lunch break, then start a program to distribute tiny knit hats to preemies in the neonatal ICU. Building an authentic brand is about infusing what you love and what you want to do into your job. Sometimes we're so consumed with our day-to-day jobs, we forget to do this. It takes innovation and creativity, but finding ways to bring your true self to your job is worth it.

YOUR DOUBT IS SHOWING:
HOW TO MAKE YOUR DOUBT A SHADOW

The first few years on the anchor desk there were constant voices in my head. As I was reading stories ranging from how to save money at a consignment sale to a triple homicide, part of me wasn't paying attention to the words because a screaming, screeching voice was telling me I wasn't good enough. I had never done this before, my peers didn't think I deserved to be here (one anchorman even told me so, to my face one day), and since I didn't sound or look like all the other anchors, it made me feel extra self-conscious. Did I use the correct em-PHA-sis on the right syl-LAB-ble? Maybe I should have crossed my arms instead of putting my palms flat on the desk? I should have ad-libbed longer about the traffic jam on Interstate 435 . . . right?

It was apparent I was suffering from a bad case of self-doubt. It caused me to question everything I did at work and was the start of that little teeth-grinding problem I mentioned in an earlier chapter. My way of coping (in addition to lots of "The Golden Girls" reruns and Arby's curly fries) was to share my self-uncertainty with others in my workplace. I'd fall into a pattern of walking off set and say to anybody with two ears, "How did the show look? Was I okay?" When the other person responded positively, I wouldn't believe it and would say, "I don't think I did very well . . ."

These attempts at feeling better about my performance and seeking self-assuredness actually had a negative effect on how my peers felt about me, and put doubt in their minds about whether or not I could do the job. The established anchors always trotted off the set after each show and went about their days as if nothing was wrong—even the ones who tripped over their words or blatantly messed up for thousands to see. Looking back today, those early newscasts were actually pretty good. Granted, I wasn't as polished back then but, if I do say so myself, was better at 23 than some anchors I've encountered at 43. In hindsight, here's what I should have done:

- **Avoid Extra Attention:** Even after more than 10 years behind the anchor desk, whenever I mispronounce a word, I silently kick myself for the gaffe and in my head say, "Dion, you doofus!" Sometimes it just slips out and I can't catch it and correct myself on-air in time. My remedy for this early on would be to circumvent any potential consequences, like getting a nastygram from an executive producer. I'd send emails apologizing for and explaining my momentary lapse in verbal mastery. More often than not, the manager never ever noticed the first time! Bringing awareness to something that doesn't really need it breeds unnecessary uncertainty.

- **Destroy the Dwelling and Dominos:** What I've trained myself to do is steamroll over the mistake and bury it in the ground. If I don't keep moving forward, the dominos start to fall. Replaying the mistake over and over again makes me lose focus and then doubt myself even more. You can bet after the John Boehner mishap, the rest of the show was a disaster. During the later stories about weather, community rallies, and traffic, my brain was somewhere else, focused on how badly I had messed up, which made me stumble over what seemed like every other word. The faster you preoccupy your brain with something else other than your mistake, the faster you can dump the uncertainty and get over it.

- **Just. Get. Better:** You can print out all the mantras you want and post them in your cubicle or on your Instagram but, why do that when you can use that time to be proactive and strengthen the actual skills needed to accomplish your job the best you can? After the John Boehner incident, I went to work just a few minutes early every day to meticulously comb through all my scripts and put them into my own words. I'd ask a producer to spell out phonetic pronunciations for names and words I didn't know. Others can tell you to do better, but you're the only one who can push yourself into making it happen. When you can then see the results of getting better, the shadows of doubt start to shrink away.

WORK AND LIFE ARE NOT A "BEST OF" OR EMMY AWARDS

How many times have you waited for weeks to get a reservation at a new restaurant that's been written up in every magazine/food blog/review site as the hottest place to dine and arrive only to be let down? There was a buzzy restaurant like that in North Carolina, which graced countless magazines and was deemed the year's "best" in the country. When I finally got in, it was good, but nothing to write home about. In fact, if you ask me today what I ate, I couldn't tell you except for the buttery, pillow-soft bread rolls with flakes of delicate gray salt sprinkled on top. A restaurant industry insider later leaked to me that the restaurant, along with another eatery on the "best" list, had hired the same public relations team to promote their business and get them as much press as possible, and that PR team had a relationship with many magazines. Coincidence?

Here's a news flash: there is no such thing as "best," as the concept is pretty subjective. Unless you're talking about math, chemistry, or something so precise that there can be a right or wrong answer, the idea of best anything is pretty silly. Just as the Italian restaurant with three Michelin stars and a $280 tasting menu appeals to gourmands, Jesse from small-town Texas, who grew up on BBQ brisket, may find the courses upon courses of tiny plates adorned with truffle shavings repulsive. It's why I take little stock in television news Emmys, Associated Press awards, or Society of Professional Journalists accolades. Sure, they're nice benchmarks to show the world you're good at your job, and I wouldn't diminish the accomplishments of those who win the awards. But isn't it more important to do quality work you're proud of every day? Plus, not having to rely on an award to justify your worth and skill means you can save the time and effort you use on trying to get recognition and instead use it on something that'll fortify your own brand and have more lasting and impactful results that directly affect your career. This way, as awards seasons come and go, you'll still have something to hold on to that's not a plaque or trophy just hanging on the wall or sitting on your desk.

Comparing yourself to others, essentially making a mental "qualifiers" list, also screws with your psyche and can self-sabotage your career. When I entered the workforce, I'd instantly start sizing myself up to any female who came into the newsroom to interview for a job. I once confronted an Asian woman and asked her brazenly, "Are you here for my job?" This was not the way to kick things off on the right foot. Looking back, I now know my jealous behavior came from not feeling confident with myself and seeing other women as a threat to my self-worth. It took a lot of therapy, soul-searching, and some pivotal moments to turn this thinking around and become a champion for other women.

CACKLE OR CRACK-UP: BUILD CONFIDENCE BY LEARNING TO LAUGH AT YOURSELF

As I wriggled out of the slightly-too-tight, coral-colored crepe dress at the end of my shift and gave a sigh of relief, something made a faint "plunk" noise as it hit the ground. I looked down and didn't see anything and continued to remove the vacuum-sealing shapeware from my torso. While bending down to pick up the nude-colored SPANX to toss them into the wicker laundry hamper, I saw it—the object that made the sound as it hit the hardwood floor.

Lying on the ground, stuck to a piece of lint, was a glistening chicken wing bone with a nubby bit of cartilage clinging to it. OMG!

I had gone to a neighborhood potluck party during my dinner break, where one of the star dishes was San Francisco's famous sweet and sticky San Tung chicken wings. Clearly, I had eaten those wings with gusto because I had, apparently, devoured them so quickly, I left a souvenir in the cowl neckline of my dress. This meant, as I anchored the 11 p.m. newscast that night, reading undoubtedly about overturned cars, a shooting, and the new

Silicon Valley startup, there was a partial chicken wing, tucked away neatly in my outfit.

Oy vey!

Once the bout of uncontrollable laughter subsided, I watched the DVR'd newscast to see if the bone was protruding anywhere, or had made a visible oily stain. There was no evidence of any chicken wing consumption on TV! It was my tasty little secret.

This could have gone one of two ways: Conventional wisdom calls for "putting your best foot forward" or "keeping up appearances," to exude the epitome of perfection to the world. Or, there's an entirely different approach. Dion's wisdom called for posting the incident, along with a screen grab of that night's newscast, on Facebook, Twitter, and Instagram. The result was several thousand viewers who laughed along with me online, who, along with colleagues, would recount tales of their own food and fashion faux pas. (Nothing brings people together like commiserating about the time you dropped an entire rack of baby back ribs, clothed in their saucy splendor, all over a wedding dress.) I suddenly went from being polished TV news lady to a real human being.

Wouldn't you rather work with a real human versus a robot or too-polished Stepford Wife? Laughter is relatable and what we seek out in a partner, or on TV and film. The ability to laugh at yourself is one way to not only cope with a mortifying incident or mix-up, but opens you up to opportunity, relatability, and brings you closer to others.

- **All Adults Are Really Just Giant Children:** Guess what? Even the most seemingly hardened adults are really just big kids. I have seen this, or maybe I should say smelled it for myself: an elevator full of grown men and women in power suits giving each other shifty-eyed smirks before bursting out in laughter after one of them passed the most foul-smelling, fermented-egg-salad fart and we were all trapped! We've all had mortifying moments! Allowing yourself to laugh at your own goofs prevents others from laughing *at* you, because they'll be laughing right *with* you. Plus, it always feels good knowing others find you amusing or entertaining.

- **The Downside of Self-Depreciation:** There's a fine line between poking fun at yourself and self-sabotage. As effective an occasional jab about something you did can be at showing transparency and relatability, doing it too often can be seen as self-loathing, and injects doubt into others as to whether you're really qualified to do the job at hand. A former anchor I worked with almost always put himself down after making a mistake, despite being in the business for more than 20 years. While it was meant to be funny and a show of modesty, many of us felt it was odd for someone to be so experienced, yet always putting himself down. It gave us the impression he had poor self-esteem, and was no longer at the top of his game.

WHAT'S MY AGE AGAIN?
(KNOW YOUR VALUE, NOT YOUR NUMBER)

"OMIGOSH, Jack, I didn't know you were that old! Happy Birth-daaaaaay! I'm exactly *half* your age! Isn't that cool?!" I practically squealed during a commercial break.

No, Dion. That is *not* cool. Reminding your coanchor that he's 46 when you're 23 is absolutely, 100 percent not cool, and 100 percent the wrong way to foster a good working environment and wish someone a happy birthday.

But at the time, I was anchoring my first weekday morning newscast, and I thought it was "cute" and what I needed to prove that I could run with the big boys. Wouldn't they be impressed I got hired to do the same job as them, but with 20+ years *less* experience?

Three women in their forties and fifties had filed a discrimination lawsuit just a few months after I was hired. While they were kind and polite to my face, we always kept conversations to cordial, greetings, and small talk. They made it pretty clear early on that our relationship would not be one of a mentoring role. I read the affidavit and understood why. There it was in black and white: my name listed as one of the "younger women" who got the weekend anchoring job, over them, because of my age.

No! That's not why I got the job! I clamored in my head. It's because I'm good at my job . . . right? The doubt set in.

Shortly after I was promoted to a Monday–Friday morning anchor position, my twice-my-age coanchor sauntered by and casually asked if I got a raise in pay. In hindsight, this was a totally inappropriate question, but I answered, thinking it was a chance to show him I belonged and didn't get hired cheap, like the lawsuit was alleging. Instead of having the confidence to shut down his question, I foolishly responded, thinking I needed to prove I was worthy with my salary. "My agent and I asked for $92,000, which we didn't quite get, but we're happy, yes!" I beamed. Said older colleague gave a tight little smile, and a curt, "Well, good. Good for you," and walked away. Little did I realize, years later, the number was actually pretty high for someone with only two years of experience in TV and probably way more than my coanchor made when he was starting out. Not long after that, when we were talking about something trivial, he suddenly spit out the stinging words, "You don't even deserve to be here!"

Making a mad dash to the restroom, wiping tears away with my sleeve, and looking like a mess, right then and there, I made two vows. One, to never tell anyone my salary again, and two, to stop telling people my age. After all, my joke is that "Asians don't raisin" (meaning, because of the extra melanin in our skin, we don't wrinkle as easily) and we could easily pass for 14 or 41, depending on hair and makeup.

Until San Francisco, I've always been the youngest person in the newscast position I held. The closest primary evening anchors in Charlotte and Tampa had to have been at least 10 years older. To me, giving off the illusion of being older would help me gain respect and not be thought of as "cheap labor."

At my current job, I dropped strategic rumors that I was 40 years old. It became such a joke in the first few months of my employment, I started pushing my age back as far as I could to see who would believe me. When our administrative assistant asked for my DOB to book a plane ticket in my name, I told her my birth year was 1964. Who lies about their age by rounding *up* a decade, let alone two decades?! It ended up being hilarious once I let her in on the joke, and I realized something: Why am I hiding my age? I'm confident and have the résumé to back it up. What would I have told my 23- and 24-year-old self? That even though my list of accomplishments was pretty bare at the time, I was there to bring energy and a new perspective to the team. I had skills of my own to bring to the table (like blogging and being super-proficient with social media which, at the time, was pretty new for a news station to do) and should have let those shine, not my age or how many digits were on my paycheck.

In a world where our older male colleagues get to wear their age like a badge of honor, while a woman's value gets branded as "tired" or "past her prime," I don't go around boasting my actual age. But on the other hand, when someone asks, I give a ballpark answer—somewhere in my thirties.

This is when we need to showcase what we bring to the table. Because your value isn't quantified by a number. It's determined by the experiences you have, how you handle them, all the while being open to learning and being unstoppable.

- **Help Others to Not Be Overshadowed:** A colleague of mine likes to remind the 20-somethings (and on occasion 30-somethings, like me) in the workplace how young they are. An occasional reference to a 1960's R&B band or a sentence starting with "You're too young to remember this . . ." is funny the first few times around. But after a while, it becomes a thinly veiled insult, insinuating you know less than they do. When this colleague decided to comment on our 24-year-old production assistant not being alive during the *Challenger* explosion, I came to her defense and said, "Just because Ashley wasn't there for the explosion, doesn't mean she can't look it up and learn about it online. She's just the perfect age and I value what she brings to the table." The young woman mouthed "thank you" in my direction. Her age, or my age at that, was never brought up again by this person. Always be willing to stand up for others who haven't learned how to showcase their own value.

YOU ARE *MORE* THAN ENOUGH
JUST THE WAY YOU ARE

For weeks leading up to the Golden State Warriors NBA Championship trip to Cleveland, my fellow teammates kept telling me how lucky I was to not only go on this assignment of a lifetime (I was already picturing myself inside the Warriors locker room with $400,000 worth of golden-dipped Moët bottles ready to be popped), but that I'd be working with Andy as my cameraman. Andy came from a journalism family. His father was a respected anchor and reporter, and Andy was an esteemed photographer, and member of the Silver Circle club, having been in the TV business more than 40 years. It was a win-win opportunity.

Kind of.

We were chatting in our rented Dodge minivan, planning our day in Cleveland, when, as soon as I mentioned taking some videos and photos for social media, he unleashed. It wasn't an angry or aggressive unleashing, but more like an impassioned pontification on the importance of journalism, and alluded to the idea that because I take selfies, I'm compromising my journalistic integrity by making me the focus of the story. Uh, at last check, taking a selfie at a basketball game was not the same as taking a selfie in front of a flag-draped casket at the funeral of a slain police officer.

For the next half hour, I listened to him explain how he was not a photographer, but a "photojournalist," and that social media, which I engaged in daily, was cheapening the craft. He grilled me on why I took so many photos and posted videos that included me in them. Among other topics he covered in his journalism sermon:

- How I should be less energetic on camera

- How I should not smile so much while anchoring

- How I have potential but was not credible to the Bay Area audience

- How he preferred my voice in real life to the one on TV

Screeeech! Hold up! You may be wondering why, after nearly half an hour of being subjected to his lecturing I did not:

A. Jump out the window

B. Kick Andy in the groin

C. Start crying like 23-year-old me usually would have

I did none of these things, because it was illogical for a man who I had just met about three hours ago to judge me like this. I took his tirade with a grain of salt. What I "should" be is me. It's what got me here in the first place.

Instead of being argumentative, this could be a teachable moment. I gave a logical example of why I took photos of myself at the Oscars (Because it's kind of the purpose of the whole awards show, and it's a *fun* evening where everyone gets dressed to get their photo taken!) and why I never posted a photo of myself let alone took one while covering a triple homicide or a court case involving an energy utility company. Andy considered himself a progressive and a champion for women. So, I asked him if he encouraged women to be themselves on-air, as they were in real life, and I explained that I believed in showing my authentic self, which is a person who smiles at stories about senior citizens breaking the world record for speed walking.

While I may not have won him over, he did not expect me to respond so candidly and I believe that gave him a level of respect, just as I respected him for expressing his criticisms to my face in a polite (albeit blunt) way, versus some of the other veterans who just talked about me behind my back. Andy even did a semi-apology the day after, saying if he pushed me too hard, I should let him know. He seemed to admire my determination not to surrender and my thought-out reasoning. These are the times when standing up for yourself can make the biggest long-term impact. You're sending a message to respectfully disagree and that you'd like to be respected. Communicating this way can be the difference between butting heads and setting a negative tone for your relationship going forward, or setting precedent that you're in this to achieve the same goals together.

- **Mental Inventory:** During these times, (or just periodically throughout the workweek) I do a mental checklist highlighting my achievements and contributions to the job at hand. It serves as a self-reminder and confidence booster and comes in handy during the times when others try to take away your self-assuredness. The same way some employers hold regular meetings to discuss positive things that have happened recently to motivate staff, this is your periodic pep talk. Even if it's a minute, when you're in the shower or while waiting for your car's oil to be changed. These moments of self-recognition help build self-assuredness over time.

- **Respect for Others Equals Respect for Yourself:** There were a lot of things I admired about Andy. His dedication to being in such a stressful, fast-paced profession for so long, lugging around heavy camera gear, and never complaining about the hard work was impressive. Because I appreciated this, I wanted him to hear why I carried myself the way I did and why I worked differently than he did. Using points from those mini pep talks to myself over the years, I was able to explain why my own methods were effective for me. It showed mutual respect and helped our relationship despite not agreeing.

- **Head-On Calm:** Whenever someone is trying to take away your worth by making overly critical comments, unwanted suggestions, or digs at the way you conduct yourself or do your job, this is not the time to stay silent and "just take it." It's a time to use logic over the inclination to feel attacked. When you remember you are steadfast in knowing your self-worth, abilities, and talents and then take it a step further to convey it to the other person calmly, it shows you're in control of who you are and sends a message that while he or she may indeed be more experienced or knowledgeable about certain subjects, he or she may not be more experienced or knowledgeable about who *you* are.

Back It Up

When I was still a student journalist working part time on the assignment desk, and as an unpaid intern at the FOX station in Hartford, Connecticut, the news director (and one of my former mentors) critiqued a story and immediately said, "Dion, how many facts do you have in this piece?" I counted none. He said it's harder to get people on board with your story when you don't have hard facts to support what you're saying. While the discussion

I had with Andy had absolutely nothing to do with stats, facts, or scientific anything, I was always ready with an answer to backup why I was, yes, a journalist, credible, and good at my job. Are there examples, scenarios, points, or figures you can use in your responses? They'll go a long way to strengthen your point of view.

A Discussion, Not a Debate

The goal is to always have a conversation, not a debate where there's shouting and confrontation. The difference between discussion and debate is that in the latter, both sides are set on their beliefs and are trying to convince their sparring partner or an audience that their side is right. Discussion is when both parties are open to new ideas. By showing empathy or understanding perspective in a discussion, using the phrase "I understand your point of view" or "I see where you're coming from" helps the other person realize you're open to moving forward . . . together.

The day after my discussion with Andy, I approached a Golden State Warriors fan in Cleveland and asked if I could interview him for our newscast. His face lit up as he exclaimed, "Hey! I saw your Tweet about being here on Twitter. How cool. Yeah, I'd be happy to talk to you!" I glanced over at Andy and gave him a sly smirk as if to say, "See? Social media can come in handy!" and couldn't help but think the corners of his mouth were ever-so-slightly turned up, too.

EMPOWER OTHERS TO EMPOWER YOURSELF (YOU CAN'T HAVE ONE WITHOUT THE OTHER)

It doesn't take throwing someone a party or blasting a praise-filled email to the entire department. (Although those things are appreciated when used for the appropriate occasion.) Empowerment happens over time, through the little things like conveying to someone else how much you value his or her work or opinions to gifting a small token of appreciation.

Embracing this concept was a process for me. I spent many years early on as a newsroom reporter/anchor full of jealousy and discomfort. Any other woman who came in for an interview became my enemy. On more than one occasion, whenever another woman came into the station, even for something as innocent as a station tour, I'd furiously start Googling her name to see if I was "better" and to pick apart her weaknesses. This behavior happened because I didn't feel good enough to stand on my own, and felt threatened instead of confident in what I could bring to the table. This was the result of encounters with those betta fish I talked about earlier in the book. Somehow, I had turned into my own version of the catty, gossiping insecure females I was surrounded by.

It wasn't until an established anchor I admired named Sonja pulled me aside and told me we all have something special to offer the world, and that there was room for all of us in the workplace that my attitude changed. When she told me she wanted to pass that message along to me and raise me up, I was floored—and grateful. She took me under her wing because it's what someone had done for her decades earlier. You'll read more about Sonja later.

SURROUND YOURSELF WITH PEOPLE WHO EMPOWER YOU

I owe a lot of my success to the people who believed in me before I believed in myself. To Laurie, the reporter who took me under her wing when I was a naive 18-year-old intern and gently encouraged me not to wear booty shorts to the station or tell people about the date I had with a 38-year-old reporter, and who also taught me that as a minority woman herself, the cards are doubly stacked against us. It was surreal to run into her out in the field more than 17 years later covering a mass shooting in Southern California, going live right beside her. I think about those who gave me a chance, then cheered me on to not just succeed, but to keep pushing beyond the level I was working at and to thrive. I owe thanks to the VP of an entire broadcasting company, who took a chance hiring me at 23 to anchor when I had never even sat in an anchor chair before. Thanks also to my coanchor Reggie, who constantly reminded me to keep my eye on the prize because I was destined for bigger things than the drama that sometimes swirled around us. These peers' encouragement empowered me to want to empower others and pass it on.

But along your journey (mine was five cities in 15 years) you'll run into these kinds of people, or you'll seek them out. But there will also be friends, family, and colleagues, who, unintentionally or not, will bring you down and do the opposite of empower—whether because it's from their own insecurities or their personality. Whatever the reason, it's your choice whether or not to let them stay and bring you down or, this will sound harsh, kick them to the curb so you can soar.

Cut Them Out and Cut the Guilt

For a while, Jasmine was part of my regular crew. A fellow morning reporter at a competing television station, we bonded over our ungodly work hours at biweekly afternoon happy hours at a local seafood joint that served a basket of fried clams for just $1.99. (Who eats fried clams on the reg living in the landlocked Midwest?)

It didn't show in the beginning, but as Jasmine and I got closer, she confided things to me which were not healthy. Not in a drug-abusing or violent or self-harming kind of way, but in a way that was mentally exhausting. She had very low self-esteem and wanted to have an affair with an older married colleague who paid attention to her. She'd complain about her salary and how it was lower than everyone else's despite her seniority. She also lamented about feeling trapped and dreamed of traveling the world, eating arancini under the Leaning Tower of Pisa and trekking the Great Wall of China. As much as I tried to be a good friend and advise her not to sleep with her coworkers, to form a strategy on how to ask for a raise, and encourage her to follow her passions, she just kept pulling me deeper into her pity party. It became draining and felt like a chore. I had gone from her friend to her therapist and this was not okay.

While it sounds terrible, I had no choice but to cut her off. She'd call me while I was out in the field to lament about trivial things like her chipped pedicure and wanting to complain about the nail technician to all the things that didn't go well in her life. I'd be 10 or 15 minutes behind on my story because I was so tangled up listening to her bemoaning and trying to be a good friend. It became a one-sided friendship—she was so up to her eyeballs in her own problems, I could never share with her my own work issues or triumphs, like being named Best Morning Anchor by a local newspaper just 10 months after I started my job. This was quite a contrast to my college bestie Iris, who yelped with joy when I called her with the exciting news. Instead of listening to Jasmine's grievances on why her career was stagnant and love life nonexistent, Iris was cheering me on from 1,200 miles away and placing ridiculous hypothetical bets on how many years it would take before I'd reach "Good Morning America" status. It was time to cut off Jasmine.

It's hard to sever a toxic relationship when the person is someone you work with day in and day out, but even more crucial so
you can keep climbing without someone keeping you down.

- **Make the Cut:** Making the decision to cut someone out
  is sometimes the hardest part because of guilt. Listening to someone is one of the best ways to show you care.
  But there's a difference between being a good friend or coworker and being someone's one-way relationship. Think
  of it this way: if someone is dragging you down with their
  problems/gripes/issues, despite knowing you've got work
  to do, it's a form of sabotage. Saboteurs don't deserve your
  time.

- **Extraction Blueprint:** Once you've made the decision to
  extract yourself from this person, you can deploy my one-
  two strategy so as not to offend yet help the person at the
  same time. This way you can remain professional and there
  is no ill-will down the road. First, let the communication
  languish. Calls get sent to voicemail. Requests to talk get
  circumvented with an excuse of being busy on a project.
  Along with the avoidance, I always try to guide the person
  toward an external solution. That solution could be therapy,
  or discussing the dragging issue with a superior or someone more appropriate. This dual-stepped technique works
  because you're sending a message that you're not interested
  but you are still vested in helping this person get help.

Looking back at those years where I did everything to suppress my Asian-ness and who I was seems pretty ridiculous. My
heritage, my personality, my way of accomplishing the day-to-day
tasks are now things I wear like a badge of pride. But I needed that

time in my life where I felt so trapped, suppressed, and insecure to get to where I am now. It's about surrounding yourself with those who will cheer you on, finding and associating with those who believe in you before you believe in yourself. It's about discovering and embracing who your true self is and allowing others in to see who that is. These things are not only crucial to being successful in your career, but in life as well.

Optics
What's on the Outside Matters More Than You Think

HE *NEW YORK TIMES* published an article in March 2018 titled, "How to Look Believable," with the subtitle "Sometimes All You Can Control Is on the Outside." A student at UC Berkeley, who alleges she was sexually assaulted by a well-known professor, wrote the piece. As she made the rounds appearing on cable news networks to tell her side of the story, she found it a struggle to balance what she wore and how she presented herself with who she was as a person, to appear credible and genuine. During the Christine Blasey Ford testimony on Capitol Hill, I was surprised at how many people were commenting on her outfit/hairstyle/overall look and then deemed her believable. Weren't her words and harrowing story enough?

That got me thinking.

In my field, I am judged on appearances on a daily basis. But it's not just appearing credible. It's presenting yourself as trustworthy, competent, or whatever impression you want to portray to the workplace when you're just starting out and don't know what you're doing. Looking the part is half the battle, and it can send the message you're ready to conquer whatever is thrown at you . . . whether or not you really are.

THE RED ON-AIR LIGHT IS ALWAYS ON

For me, being ready meant that when a veteran anchor fell ill with a case of vertigo just 15 minutes before the newscast, the boss scanned the newsroom to see who was available to substitute. Despite having never anchored a weekday newscast in my life, my makeup and hair were already clean and styled, so I looked the part. With one point and a nod, I was in. The audience responded so well that I ended up getting a promotion shortly thereafter. A more seasoned colleague who was also in the newsroom at the time, hair in curlers, missed out and ended up leaving the TV business a few years later. Being ready was essentially an audition I only got because I was primed for it without even knowing.

It sounds so darn simple, but you'd be amazed at how many women come to work clutching their makeup bags and hair styling products, looking like they just rolled out of bed. Sure, you may have time to put yourself together in the restroom before the morning client meeting . . . but imagine what could happen if you took that few minutes at home to prepare your physical self?

This part of the book isn't about fashion and how to achieve a killer makeup "face beat," but, rather, it's about setting yourself up for success. Being ready and giving the appearance of being prepared (even when you're not) can go a long way. After all, when opportunity knocks, there is no makeup artist or hair stylist to get you ready. It's all on you.

- **Your Go-Bag Only Goes so Far:** Reporters have go-bags always packed, in case of breaking news that requires them to go out of town and stay overnight somewhere. They include rainboots for floods, parkas for snow, and all the necessary toiletries. While having this bag handy is great, on a daily basis you need to be ready to go as soon as you're on the clock. I don't necessarily mean having a full face of makeup, but think about the optics if you're rushing into a meeting, lint-roller in hand and swishing Listerine because you decided to get ready on the fly instead of at home?

- **Better Version of *You*:** The whole "dress for the job you want" saying is total BS. If you're a cashier at a supermarket, you'd look pretty silly wearing a three-piece suit. Instead, it's about creating the best version of the job you have. Ask yourself how you can elevate your exterior to make someone trust what you bring to the table. Is the $30 investment of getting your hair blown out before pitching a high-powered developer on your business worth it? If I were that developer, I'd want to spend my hundreds of thousands of dollars on someone who looks the part: high end and put together, not sloppy and unprepared.

CREATE THE ILLUSION OF BEING READY: FROM GREECE TO DC

Remember the Athens to DC problem-solving incident? Well, tucked into my beat-up carry-on Tumi suitcase, alongside the strappy sandals, off-the-shoulder beachwear, and caftans, was an essential piece of hardware: my IFB, the tiny molded earpiece device that could be attached to any standard industry audio jack to allow the user to hear whatever was going on. (Think of it as a single tiny custom earphone.) While an IFB may be like a judge's gavel, a nurse's stethoscope, or a carpenter's tape measure, or any other crucial piece of equipment needed for work, it's the last thing one thinks of while lounging by an infinity pool on the mountainside of a Greek caldera. But it came in handy when I got the call to go to Washington, DC. I was ready to go. Could the photographer have gotten one for me? Of course, but the fact that I had it with me was even mentioned in a companywide email that got sent out, recognizing employees who went above and beyond their job description. Two plastic ounces, smaller than a stick of gum, was all it took to show off my dedication to being a team player.

- **Anticipate the Needs of Others:** One of my favorite baristas at Blue Bottle coffee starts my order before we finish exchanging our hellos. Even if he doesn't remember what we talked about last week, getting my hot oat milk latte ready early before I even pay gives off the impression he's going the extra mile to make my experience better. The same concept applies at your workplace. You may never have to actually fulfill what someone else needs, but wanting to, even if it's as simple as picking up someone's project at the printer and swinging it by his or her desk, goes a long way. Trust me, it'll make you look really good.

- **Availability:** While I don't advocate being glued to your phone at all times and answering your work phone during your days off, the optics of taking a call or on occasion answering an important email at 11 p.m. is that you're working hard. A quick three-minute chat or tapping out of an email during the commercial break of "The Bachelor" isn't going to ruin your evening. But it will show whoever is at the end of the line that you're present and "on it," even when you're off.

- **Timing Can Be Everything:** As a kid, my mom was obsessed with being early. A flight at the airport meant being there three hours ahead of schedule. Appointments at the doctor—we would be leafing through tattered issues of *People* magazine in the waiting room at least 45 minutes beforehand. (Yet the doctor was always late, meaning we were really waiting more like 90 minutes!) Maybe her idea of being ready was a tad excessive, but it gave me the discipline later in life to always be on time. You don't even have to do anything special—just show up. That, in itself, sends a clear message. When a coanchor of mine regularly came in an hour late, it gave the optics of not caring about the rest of the team. Producers would have to stop what they were doing to search the building for him, only to come up short. It made me feel disrespected because I was the one making calls and working on assignments since I was the only on-air person there to do it. Your ability to be early will signal to the rest of your work squad that you're there for them.

SKITTLES SIGNATURE: FIND YOUR LOOK

When a writer for *Glamour* magazine reached out to me about a feature in an upcoming article about women's "work uniforms," after noticing my trademark on-air style of bright, solid colors, I realized the power my clothes could have. My "uniform" was a reflection of who I was, my energy and boldness, which set me apart from a sea of gray, black, and shades of brown.

It all started when a manager told me, in order to work at his station, I'd have to dress like a packet of Skittles, meaning rainbow colors only. This, at first, sounded utterly absurd. Did the tropical fruit colors count as well? What if the Wrigley company decided to jump on the bandwagon of incorporating detoxifying black charcoal in its candies? After trying it for a few months (thanks to my Rent the Runway unlimited subscription, which allowed me to have an endless spectrum of colors for less than the price of buying one outfit), I understood the mandate. (He had just communicated the benefits of wearing Skittles colors all wrong.) It was twofold: not only did the jewel tones and eye-catching colors help draw attention and get the audience to listen, they weren't distracted by patterns and embellishments. This consistency helped me stand out. Before viewers remembered my last name, they knew me as the lady on the news who wore radiant colors and that gave me confidence to focus on my job, not on what I was wearing.

Granted, if you're a funeral home director, wearing hot pink probably isn't the best choice. But ask yourself: Are there components to your appearance that you love and make you feel confident? Ariana Grande wouldn't be rocking that signature high ponytail everyday if she didn't like it or it didn't make her feel like a pop star. Whether it's a piece of jewelry or the way you tie your shoelaces, make a statement about who you are with each item you choose. Being known for being put together and doing it in your own way sends the ultimate message: I'm good at my job and ready to show you how good.

OPTICS SOS

My first lesson in visual suitability came when 18-year-old intern Dion thought it would be cute to wear a pastel blue United Colors of Benetton belly shirt (At the time, I thought it was so fancy and exclusive, since it took me two days of work as a supermarket cashier to pay for it!) and low-riding white denim cutoff shorts to the office. Less than 15 minutes after bounding into the newsroom with a drink holder full of coffees, a reporter, who had taken me under her wing, pulled me aside and asked if I had a change of clothes. Too bad I didn't because less than 15 minutes later, the manager on duty saw my lame excuse for work attire and I was sent home for the day. That was the day I made the decision to always dress professionally for whatever job I had. The next day, when I donned my best button-up shirt and black dress pants to the newsroom, the crews allowed me to tag along and shadow the reporter. I even was able to attempt recording a few practice on-camera segments for my college résumé. I'd later learn presenting professionally was just the beginning. It's about helping others present themselves suitably for their surroundings. Because the optics of others in your organization only help—or hurt—your own.

Looking back now, that reporter was trying to give me a heads-up and prevent me from developing a reputation before I was even employed. How would it have looked for her if she went out in public with me by her side, clad in that outfit more appropriate for clubbing rather than attending a court hearing? Her own reputation would have suffered. So, when years later I encountered a similar situation with a colleague, I knew what had to be done.

Hope was the kind of reporter who didn't need to be told how to dress in the office. Her dresses and suits were always immaculately dry-cleaned and on trend. Experience-wise she was a little greener than the rest of the team, but she made up for it by presenting herself well and always being eager to learn. That is, until the storm of the season arrived.

When a reporter gets deployed on storm coverage, their go-bag is usually filled with wild weather gear like an umbrella, waterproof boots, and a rain jacket. (If you're one of those over-the-top network reporters on a 24-hour cable channel, perhaps add in some goggles for a dose of drama and good measure.) But when Hope went out, she refused to wear any sort of severe weather gear. It would be downpouring, but for the few moments she was live on television, she'd be in a sleeveless pink dress, nothing over her head, and looking like she had made zero attempt at being ready for Mother Nature's beating. It was ridiculous because by the time her story aired, and she was live on the back end of the segment, her shiny, usually kempt cascading red hair resembled a matted-down drowning rat. Let's not even talk about the strappy sandals. Something had to be done. Not only because viewers were messaging *me* asking what was up with her poor choice in attire, but because that saying of being only as strong as your weakest (in this case, wettest) link truly applied here. The whole news organization looked ridiculous.

- **Finding the Root Cause:** Before assisting in Hope's situation, or any optics-related scenario, it was vital to find out why she avoided wearing rain gear in the first place. Was it vanity? Perhaps she didn't have any and wasn't comfortable with asking the promotions department for a station-logoed weatherproof coat. Maybe it was for some obscure reason like she was allergic to synthetic materials found in umbrellas! This can be done through asking others who work with the person. It'll help determine what steps to take next.

- **The Roundabout Comment or Question:** After some inquiry, the jury (my coworkers) was split. The general consensus was either Hope didn't cover enough weather at her previous job and just didn't know better, or that she was intentionally avoiding the water-repellent baseball caps and hoods for vanity's sake. So, when Hope showed up to work the next day, without making it seem like an ambush, I asked how her story shoot went. When she responded that it went well, but that the weather was terrible, I offered to lend her my own rain gear next time. She said she had her own but appreciated the offer. The key to making this technique effective is to not ask a question out of the ordinary that would arouse suspicion of malicious intentions.

- **Casual Situational Suggesting:** Without wanting to sound like a know-it-all and instruct Hope to forget about looking cute and instead appear more weather-savvy, I decided to seize a completely unrelated moment to drop a casual suggestion, so she could connect the dots. This way, I felt, she would want to put on severe weather gear on her own accord. One day, when the station was at a volunteer trash-pickup day at a local elementary school that served underprivileged children, I rounded up a group of on-air talent and students, so we could all take a photo together.

Hope jumped at the chance but asked frantically, "Can you guys give me 10 minutes? I don't have any makeup on and I want to change my shirt!" (What did I say earlier about being ready before you come to work?!) Not only couldn't we wait because there was a tight schedule to adhere to, but why should she change out of her station T-shirt and be the only one in a pressed white button-up? My casual reply was, "This one's about the kiddos! Let's all look like we fit in with them! The dirt on our shirts looks authentic, like we've been working!" Something must've clicked because, sure enough, during the next storm there she was, not only clad in a rainproof hat and coat but with full-on waders like the Gorton's Fisherman, which allowed her to splash in puddles and access areas she never could have in her Jimmy Choo pumps and dress. The key to deploying this strategy with a colleague is to make a comment indirectly but about a similar circumstance when the time is right. Since helping others with their optics may not be as big a priority as, say, making sure your own presentation to the world is on point, it's okay not to get immediate results. It's a process— one you can seize when the time is just right.

Of course, it's unfair to judge anyone for their appearance . . . but we all know it happens every day. Instead of railing against that (admittedly unfair) truism, use that energy to be the best whatever-you-are! Are you selling real estate? You don't have to drive a late-model luxury car to instill confidence in your clients, but a potential buyer will respond one way if you're driving a beat-up old clunker and a very different way if you show them houses from the comfort of your clean, detailed, and comfortable car. If you're in a customer service position, taking the time to make sure your uniform—whatever it is—is clean and pressed and your hands are well groomed (no polish that looks like it should have been removed a month ago) will let customers know you are a conscientious person they can rely on.

The secret to the power of optics in your career journey is to embrace the fact that people really do judge a book by its cover.

Fail Your Way Forward
Sometimes It Takes One Step Back to Bound Light-Years Forward

ECAUSE OF THE business I'm in, I've probably experienced more failing than the average employed person. But this part of the book isn't filled with Kelly Clarkson song lyrics about what doesn't kill you makes you stronger, or motivational sayings emblazoned on posters with bald eagles soaring over the Rocky Mountains. It's about putting the brain-spinning, shock-and-awe, bawl-your-eyes out, knee-jerk reactions aside and learning to process setbacks in a way that leaves you poised to grab the next opportunity.

When my company in Tampa laid off what seemed like the entire 11 p.m. newscast, I took the news hard. Even though I knew from the moment the news director uttered the words, "We're going to part ways," it didn't have anything to do with my own performance, my skills, or how I interacted with my team, I was devastated. It felt like a betrayal. How was I supposed to act like everything was coming up roses on-air for the remaining time I was there?

Of course, as you have likely experienced yourself, setbacks can include so much more than getting let go from your job. There are the day-to-day mistakes, incorrect handling of situations, and unexpected bad outcomes. It's the way you process these bumps in the road, or seemingly enormous catastrophes, that'll shape your career going forward.

PREPARE FOR WORKPLACE ARMAGEDDON

The idea of preparing to be laid off, even when you just start a job, sounds paranoid. But hear me out. If the Bureau of Labor Statistics reports the average employee stays at his or her job just 3.2 years, doesn't that mean you should always be prepared for what's next? Compare that to the "lifers" of our parents' or grandparents' generation, where after graduation they'd hold one job for the rest of their lives. Preparing for what's next, no matter how secure you are in your current position, will keep you light on your feet and on top of your game because you'll be ready for whatever setbacks come your way. I've been doing it my whole career, and when I was laid off in Tampa, it helped me land in a bigger market at a better station in a city I love.

Even after being named one of the top leaders in television by the trade publication *Broadcasting and Cable*, winning my station's digital media star award twice, and being at the helm of a number one rated newscast, I should have felt invincible. But I knew I wasn't. Nobody is invincible. It's a lesson I learned when my contract in Charlotte was coming to an end and it was time to find another job to advance my career. My confidence was at an all-time high with dreams of big stations with big paychecks. "Good Morning America," here I come! Three years earlier, when I was going from Kansas City to Charlotte, the job search was a cakewalk. Back then, I was 26 and being courted by major market cities like Dallas, Boston, Chicago, and Miami. Even a recruiter for one of the networks wanted me to interview for an anchor job on their early morning national newscasts. (Obviously, I didn't get that gig, but was flattered nonetheless.) This experience gave me a false sense of security when, in 2013, the TV landscape had changed dramatically. There were fewer high-profile television jobs available because of an influx of other ways to consume media like through apps, on social media, and YouTube. Salaries were going down, and I suddenly found myself overqualified for half the positions available. It took twice as long to find a job that didn't tick all the boxes off my dream gig wish list while still providing me with a nice salary.

So, how do you prepare for a potential layoff? The best way to approach it is by not making it a time-consuming process, but rather a task you do in manageable bits and pieces as you go.

- **Everything Update:** For me, this means keeping samples of my on-air work—clips from out in the field reporting to anchoring breaking news. It's a lot easier to save and glean these work samples as you go versus going back into the archives and thinking back to what work you've done, trying to scramble as you get booted out the door. This could also mean saving email addresses and phone numbers, and projects and materials you think illustrate what you do best and will impress down the road. Setting reminders to periodically update your résumé, LinkedIn profile, and cover letter also come in handy, so if you do end up leaving your company unexpectedly, you can spend more time on the hunt versus gathering everything you need.

- **Forever Networking:** Sometimes when things are going smoothly at work we get complacent and we feel like there's no need to network because we know enough people in our industry, or we put relationship building at the bottom of our priorities list because we just get busy. But the truth of the matter is, when you find yourself laid off or in need of help these are the people you'll be calling on to help. It's much easier to make those phone calls or to reach out when you're already at the top of their mind, instead of having to explain, "Hey, remember me from that conference in Baltimore back in 2018? Yeah, I need a favor." This applies not only to in-person relationships but online, too. LinkedIn is not only my favorite tool to keep up with people professionally, it's something easy and can be done when you're in a time crunch. Posting regular updates on career achievements, projects, and overall lessons learned on the job takes minutes and keeps you exposed to your online network.

- **Side Hustling:** Remember how earlier, in Chapter 7, I asked you what makes you happy, because it's crucial in how to make a name for yourself? That question doesn't only apply to personal branding. What makes you happy can also translate, and in my opinion, *should* translate into a side hustle, AKA a secondary income stream. Whether it's making jam to sell at the farmers market or something larger scale, like reselling National Hockey League tickets online, having a secondary passion project has benefits for one's creativity that may not be fulfilled at work and at the same time brings in income. Even if the goal of a side hustle isn't to replace your full-time job income, knowing it's there and available to you can bring comfort when setback strikes.

I SAW THE SIGN
(ACE OF BASE WAS ONTO SOMETHING)

Part of being able to find dignity and strength to move forward comes from analyzing and making logical sense of what happened. Being prepared for a looming layoff or workplace disaster can also give you a head start in preparing for your next move. In hindsight, I really should have seen my own layoff coming. Just months earlier, the older staffers were offered early retirement packages. Promotional segments for my newscasts were few and far between, and a whole crop of job openings with much lower starting salaries popped up out of what seemed like nowhere. That was the higher-ups' way of stealthily communicating changes were on the way for everyone and I should have listened to my gut that something was very, very wrong.

- **Use Your Intuition and Follow the Clues:** Journalists second-guess almost everything we're presented with. It's part of the territory to look past face value and dig to find the real story. Even if you're being told you're doing great at your job, take note of things that are out of the ordinary, even if they seem small. Did you get left out of a special planning meeting or a big project? Are your colleagues getting assigned tasks you're usually in charge of? Do you see an abnormally high number of job postings for your organization? If managers are acting differently toward you, either in a friendly way or avoiding conversations, perhaps you're not being paranoid. You're looking for clues that could mean the difference between getting blindsided or being prepared for whatever happens next.

LAID OFF. REDISTRIBUTED. CANNED. WHATEVER YOU CALL IT: YOU'RE FIRED

One of my mentors once told me, "If you haven't been laid off or canned, or your contract not renewed, then you haven't really lived." Chances are, it'll happen to you at some point in your career. In fact, a 2017 study by Rutgers University's John J. Heldrich Center for Workforce Development showed one in five workers in the United States has been laid off in the past five years. You can prepare all you want, but how you respond to being laid-off and the way you behave the rest of your time at your job is just as important as getting hired in the first place.

Don't get me wrong. If you're caught stealing reams of paper from the Xerox machine to sell on eBay or are constantly showing up late and not pulling your weight, then yeah, maybe you deserve to be fired. But more often than not, the decision to lay someone off isn't personal and is completely out of your control. What you can control is your mindset: you are on the losing end of something totally circumstantial that you have no control over and no matter what you did can't change.

So how do you function when you're asked to train your replacement? Look your boss in the eye and have a conversation?

The psychological toll can be so much higher than the loss of salary! In my case, I had to pretend nothing was wrong and do it all while smiling and on camera for the whole market to see. Here's how I did it.

How to Handle a Layoff with Class and Dignity: Holly's Cake

One day after an anchor was laid off at my television station in Florida, the receptionist hauled a beautiful, towering four-layer chocolate fudge cake into the newsroom. The accompanying card read something to the extent of "Thanks for the memories!" and was signed with a flowing, cursive "H," which stood for Holly.

Word was, Holly took the news of her layoff like a champ. Her expression was like the emoji with a straight line for a mouth: deadpan the entire time as our boss broke the news and proceeded to inform her he had to leave in order to make his Thursday afternoon tee time. After we all joked about the cocoa confection being possibly laced with arsenic, my team dug in and collectively began scooping forkfuls into our mouths like famished barbarians. It wasn't until after the chocolatey carbs and the sugar-coma began to set in that it occurred to us, either Holly was the sweetest woman on the planet for having the grace to be laid off and send over a cake . . . or she was sending a wry message essentially saying since she was laid off and not given a proper send-off, she was giving herself her own send-off with a decadent, fudge "F-U."

I decided she was doing both, and silently applauded her actions in my head. *Yasss* anchor queen, *yasss*!

Holly's cake was the opposite of my own experience when I was let go three years into a four-year deal in Tampa Bay. My company had just purchased another media group and was looking to make some major changes in how television news was presented. They wanted to appeal to Millennials and a younger, more lucrative demographic. They thought it would be done by using slang, covering trending topics from Facebook, and doing more entertainment, TMZ-style news. The changes were sweeping, and frankly most of us didn't fit the mold. Sorry, but I'm not a comedian, a YouTube star, or someone who calls criminals "scumbags" on the air. Ethics and storytelling reign supreme in my book.

When the news was broken to me on a Tuesday, my emoji face couldn't be further from the straight-line mouth Holly so classily exhibited. My expression was three emojis at once: the exploding brain emoji, the waterfall of tears devastated emoji, and the green vomiting emoji.

The sudden shock, anxiety, panic, anger, and devastation were too much to bear. My hands and arms went numb, and the executive assistant had to rush in with a frozen towel to bring feeling back to my body. How could my employer praise me six months earlier for having the best social media numbers and for my dozens of public appearances speaking at schools and doing community outreach, then kick me to the curb? I felt betrayed and powerless and made no effort to hide it.

What happened to all the "reacting 101" advice I doled out in Chapter 1? Tailoring my emotions for the situation at hand? Yeah . . . I forgot all about it!

The good part about this was, I think my boss and the HR manager who sat across the shiny walnut executive table felt some kind of pity for my pathetic meltdown. Their emotionless, hard faces softened into a "Sorry, not sorry" half-apology expression as they sent me home for the day and offered me the rest of the week off so I could decompress and digest the news.

Not only did I digest, I decided I would give myself the rest of the day to pity party, calling my agent (who was vacationing in the Caribbean but made time to listen to my tearful moaning), my best friends, and closest family, all while eating copious amounts of butter-coated pasta and full-fat cheese puffs. Then, I would get back on my feet and never let them see me sweat.

- **Pity Party It Up (Just Not Forever):** There's a time where feeling sorry for yourself is completely, 100 percent a-okay. Allowing yourself to wallow in your own sadness gives you time to take all the feelings of loss, anger, and betrayal and get them out of your system. It gives you time to hit rock bottom and find the motivation to get up off the couch and back in the game. There's a point where commiserating with yourself and friends about your situation becomes so pathetic, your brain automatically kicks into recovery mode to get you back on your feet (unless you're like a friend of mine who has been on a continuous eight-year pity party—he sucks the life out of most real parties).

I think part of the reason why my boss offered to let me take the rest of the week off (don't believe the myth workers are only fired on a Friday, mine was a Tuesday) was partially because he didn't want to be reminded of the sniffling/tear-stained employee he had just broken. But I had made a commitment to speak to an elementary school the next day about, ironically enough, resilience when faced with challenges. In their case, bullying. So, instead of taking the rest of the week off, I made the presentation, came in early, and shot a bonus story that day. I ramped up my social media even more. Not only did I want to prove that my departure was going to be a loss for the company, I was going to leave my mark and go out on top. My class and grace weren't going to be a chocolate fudge cake, but me kicking as much ass as I could, acting as if nothing was wrong and setting myself up for something even greater ahead.

- **Talk Class, Not Trash:** As my colleagues were called one by one to the general manager's office in the subsequent days after my own layoff and were alerted their services would no longer be needed, the grumblings about our boss and station started percolating. By commiserating together, we became closer than ever, bending over backwards to help one another find a job and triumph after our setback. This was our coping mechanism. But when anybody in the public, or potential employers, asked us about our television station, we chose to emphasize the positives and never back talk our company for making this decision. Trash talking is seen as a reflection of your behavior on a regular basis, not just once. A recruiter even pointedly asked me how I felt about my news director and the way I was let go. Knowing this was a test, I responded diplomatically that I didn't particularly appreciate the fashion in which we were all alerted but held no ill will toward my superiors, because they obviously were tasked with following through on a companywide edict. The recruiter called my agent the very same day to say how pleased she was to hear I didn't hold a grudge and that my show of respect and stamina would be positively looked upon.

- **Knock, Knock, Who Gets Let In?** While getting laid off isn't anything to be ashamed of, it's key to allow only your core group in on what you're going through. My core group (or "squad," as the cool kids say) was vital in helping me get back on my feet and helping with the job hunt. This is the group of people in your network you can count on after a career disaster. Not the ones who say, "Reach out if you ever need anything" and leave you high and dry. I mean the people who've got your back and would offer you a room under their roof if you suddenly were homeless. The people who don't just say, "I'll see what I can do" but instead say, "I got this." The ones who would keep your secrets even if it meant they'd get in trouble themselves for not spilling the beans. It was this group who helped me make calls or reach out to television stations across the country where they knew the managers. Setting these parameters helps you stay focused and able to exert energy with those who deserve it.

THE ULTIMATE MOTIVATOR: DAN

Remember that journalism workshop I hosted with Dan Rather? Not that he was in my squad, but I trusted his judgment and advice explicitly. His point of view would be different from the guidance from the rest of my inner circle. My friends are accomplished in their own ways, but only Dan can call himself one of the original "Big Three" nightly news anchors, along with competing legends Peter Jennings and Tom Brokaw. I sent Dan an email two days after I got the news. Following is part of his email response:

> I encourage you to believe in yourself, believe in your vision of what news should be and what kind of anchor/reporter you want to be. I do think that if you are smart (and a little lucky) and are steadfast, steady and determined that you can make a difference. Especially if you fear not. Don't let them scare you.

You're too good at what you do not to do well wherever you practice your craft.

Good luck. Godspeed. I'll be pulling for you.

Courage,

Dan Rather

For weeks I carried those words with me on a tiny strip of paper in my wallet. Now, I still carry those words, but in transcended form. They've become words I believe in and apply to everything I do.

- **Who Is Your Dan Rather?** Nothing is as big a motivator as when someone you look up to puts their faith in you when it feels like your team/company/the world doesn't see your value. Even if you don't have a mentor or someone like Dan, what's stopping you from reaching out or seeking some kind of guidance from someone you admire and strive to be like?

- **Drop the Right Line:** Since the person you're reaching out to may be the president of a company, a celebrity, or someone not as accessible as the average person, you'll have to use a bit of perseverance. When I'm on the hunt to interview someone who is high profile, I start with LinkedIn, and message him or her directly through the pro feature, which goes directly into the person's email. Or, I'll find the name of his or her assistant by scouring Google or reach out to someone else in the same network. A short, concise message, not a rambling oh-woe-is-me lament with too many details, more often than not gets a response.

It may take a while and you will undoubtedly fail, but just like finding a job, all it takes is one "yes."

By handling the layoff with class and confiding in the right people (versus expressing my bitterness and feelings of betrayal to anybody who would listen or writing an anonymous blog about how awfully my employer treated me) I not only healed, but I had 100 percent sparkling reviews when potential employers made reference calls about me. In the end, this led to a job in a bigger city that's a better fit.

SETBACK IN STRIDE
(CHANGE YOUR PERSPECTIVE)

When I was 27 and promoted to the main anchor position at my station in Charlotte, I should have yelled from the rooftops when my boss broke the news. My career trajectory had happened much faster than I could have ever dreamed of. The face of an entire television station! These were positions so coveted, the primary anchor usually rode out the rest of his or her remaining career at the station. How exciting! But instead of beaming and furiously nodding my head in acceptance, tears instantly poured from my eyes. They weren't the happy kind either. They were overwhelmed tears. The only thing I could think of was how the woman I'd be replacing would take the news . . . and how I would fill her shoes.

Sonja was known as the mother of our newsroom. She was kind and gentle with a calm demeanor, which translated on-air and made her wildly popular with the audience. She led by example: organizing baby showers for expecting coworkers, and showing up early or leaving late whenever it was necessary. Plus, she was such a good listener she could have set up a booth in the parking lot and moonlighted as a drive-through therapist between newscasts. Sonja had been at the helm of the 11 p.m. newscast for decades and had deep roots in the Charlotte community. After all, her entire family hailed from the Queen City, and her father was the first African American mayor. Now, she'd be anchoring the afternoon and early newscasts, known loosely in television as the #2 anchor spot. Not #1, where she had reigned for almost more years than I had been alive.

The next day when I rounded the corner from the hallway to the makeup room with warp speed, I nearly body slammed with Sonja. Here I was, clutching my XXL jumbo-sized hairspray and hair dryer, looking as pale as if I had seen a ghost. I wailed, "Sonja, I'm so, so sorry! Please don't think I'm taking your job! Please don't hate me!" Immediately, in her motherly, compassionate way she wrapped her arms around me in a great big hug, the same way she did on my first day at the station. She then stepped back, hands on my shoulders, looked me in the eye, and said words I will never forget.

"Dion, you're not taking my job! I'm happy for you! We all go through seasons in life, and this is going to be a new chapter for me. It's *your* time to shine! Plus, now I get to go home and eat dinner with my family at night."

This was the most mind-boggling, relieving, and enlightening experience ever. In those 30 seconds, I learned how being secure in who you are, your abilities, and what you have to offer the world can give you perspective and help you see the positives of setback and how it may not really be a setback. One day, I aspire to be my own version of Sonja.

- **See the Positives When You're Stuck in the Negative:**
Sometimes we are so clouded by a setback, like a missed
promotion or demotion, we don't look at the fringe benefits. An experienced producer friend of mine was just passed
up for a coveted 11 p.m. time slot in lieu of the 6 p.m. newscast. While he said he was disappointed, he told me the
6 p.m. position would not only allow him the ability to be
home with his family at the end of the night (versus getting
home at well past midnight) but that it came with perks like
medical benefits and an additional week of vacation. Ask
yourself if this setback is actually a blessing in disguise and
the kick in the pants you need to chase your real dreams.

THE PHILADELPHIA INCIDENT: LEARN PERSPECTIVE (THE THREE CS AND DODGING THE BULLET)

It was the spring of 2013, and I had just gotten in the back of a taxi
(ridesharing wasn't yet a "thing") and called my husband. I told
him we should start looking at places to live in Philadelphia. The
interview for a very big job (one that, in hindsight, was a bit of
a reach) had gone so swimmingly smooth there was no way this
wasn't in the bag. First, a flawless two-hour anchor audition complete with ad-libbed breaking news about a fake Apache helicop-
ter making an unexpected landing. There was instant chemistry
with the people I met and one of the managers even told me which
neighborhoods to live in. But the clincher: the VP of news telling me not to accept any jobs until she had a chance to check with
corporate and call my agent. The feeling of Brotherly Love was
running through my veins and I couldn't wait to eat apple cider

donuts in the fall, have regular lunch dates with friends at Reading Terminal Market, and run up the stairs of the art museum to the *Rocky* theme song.

As the weeks went by, my agent and I were continuously encouraged with the request not to sign another contract, not to extend at my current station, nor respond to other possible offers. Insiders I had met during the interview told me there were only two other people in serious contention, but I had made the biggest impression on the staff.

Then one day, nearly two months after that glorious interview, my future seemingly solidified and my goodbye email already crafted (okay, maybe I jumped the gun on that one) I got the call while out running errands. The station had decided to go with someone else. A woman from a smaller market who was blonde, white, and looked very similar to the woman she was replacing.

Spirit crushed, there I was, feeling like I did as a child again, asking myself why I wasn't a blonde white woman instead of who I was. Had I just lost again because of what I looked like? My legs gave way and I sunk into the driver's seat and sat in the parking lot of my local Target long enough to alarm the rent-a-cops who even knocked on the window asking if I was okay. The red-and-white bag containing floor cleaner and toothpaste was still in my hand.

For months I took the news like the opposite of Sylvester Stallone. A loser. My headspace was constantly occupied by an endless loop of reliving the interview. Did I do something wrong? Was my ad-lib not comprehensive enough? Maybe I should have dyed my hair blonde. But the only blonde Asians in TV news seemed to be in Los Angeles! While I knew the business was subjective and the decision was probably completely out of my control, the rejection still sucked, and I thought about it constantly. It wasn't until months later that a mentor told me this particular station ownership group was notorious for having their corporate bigwigs make the hiring decisions. It didn't matter what the staff at the station thought of me, it was out of their control and had been from the beginning.

This not only kept me from going off the deep end, it also taught me an important lesson.

- **The Three Cs: You didn't create it. You didn't cause it. You can't change it.** Remembering these things can help you not only cope but make sense of what happened and bring you closure. You know the feeling of getting dumped for no reason or even worse, ghosted? There may never be an answer as to why it happened, but understanding these three concepts can help you come to terms with, and get over, a setback.

- **Ask if You've Dodged a Bullet:** Five years after I didn't get the job I thought I was a shoo-in for, I was shocked to learn most of the on-air talent I had met during my interview were gone. After asking a couple of acquaintances from a journalism convention who worked at the station why there had seemed to be such a large exodus of employees in recent months, they relayed some of the station's dysfunctions to me. One even told me I had "dodged a bullet" by not getting the job. As much as I wanted the Philly role at the time, I realized, in hindsight, maybe what you think you want isn't all it's cracked up to be after all. Shortly after, I was offered a job as the early evening anchor at a station in Tampa Bay. Philadelphia soon became a distant memory, as I traded the cheesesteaks and the Liberty Bell for stone crabs and sandy beaches. While it wasn't quite what I thought I wanted, it was an excellent career move.

BIGGER, BRIGHTER, BADDER
(MAKE MORE THAN ONE DOOR OPEN)

The saying "when one door closes, another one opens" is fine. But when you encounter a career setback, it's time to watch some YouTube tutorials of "This Old House," find the materials, and *make* your own door. This can be through hustling contacts or thinking outside the box. When a young, homeless web developer named David Casarez lost his job in the summer of 2018, he stood on a street corner with a sign that said, "HUNGRY 4 SUCCESS TAKE A RESUME." He ended up with more than 200 job offers, and landed a permanent job about a month later.

- **What Can *You* Do?** I get that David's strategy was beyond unorthodox and not realistic for most people. But how can you push the envelope a bit to create your own door? Years before the Marie Kondo tidying phenomenon was a Netflix hit, Jenny, a woman who is now my friend after I did a story on her, was working a miserable finance job but loved tidying in her spare time. She tracked down Marie at a book signing and basically convinced her team to hire her as an unpaid assistant, so she could learn the method. That led to a paid job. To some, this may seem outrageous, but Jenny had nothing to lose and was ten times happier than when chained to her desk crunching numbers all day.

You Just *Never* Know
(How I Got Here and How You'll Get There)

Forget Six Degrees of Kevin Bacon. It's more like two degrees when it comes to your career, no matter the industry. There are almost

326 million people living in the United States. Yet, why is it I could be on a street corner in New York City and catch the eye of an ex-boyfriend I haven't seen in 15 years who just happened to be getting in a cab? Or wandering the streets of Tokyo and see an old neighbor of mine from Boston? While I can't explain the science or the mathematical odds of this happening, I can tell you the world is a whole lot smaller than even the saying implies . . . and you can use it to your advantage.

When I asked a former agent of mine about a job opening in Los Angeles, he pretty much shut down the idea immediately, using the excuse that stations there liked to hire native Californians to read the news. Having never lived in California would be a black mark on my résumé. While, yes, it's a benefit in the TV industry to work where you grew up (nothing helps one's popularity like being a hometown kid) there are plenty of people who work in cities they had no affiliation with. (I mean, Oprah freaking Winfrey is from Kosciusko, Mississippi, population just about 6,891.) Good thing I didn't listen to that agent (and subsequently fired him), because guess what? Five years later, I'm working in California. What helped me make up for my lack of West Coast ties was the wide and wild web of people I knew throughout the years but had no idea would play a role in getting me to where I wanted to be.

When my agent looked into a job for me in San Francisco, I knew despite my accomplished résumé, there would be hundreds of applicants and I needed an inside edge in order to rise to the top of the applicant pool.

This is when my networking skills and willingness to *ask* went into overdrive.

While talking to Iris, my reporter bestie in Syracuse about my job search, she dropped a bombshell. Her photographer, whom she worked with every day for 10 years, had dated a woman who was now a news director in San Francisco. Turns out, it was my current news director! He also worked with my former coanchor in Charlotte as well at my station in Tampa before moving to Syracuse. She started shrieking and five minutes later, her photographer was on the phone with my now boss.

This got me thinking. Who else is out there who could be of help in my quest? Here's a few strategies on how to get started:

- **Snoop Sensibly:** If the Iris/photographer example wasn't kismet enough, I just happened to be doing some background research on the managers at the station in San Francisco and noticed a newly retired photographer I used to work closely with during public appearances. That person was a first-level connection on LinkedIn with the news director. Since Larry and I had a good relationship, I had no shame in calling him to ask what their connection was. Turns out Larry was a mentor to her as she was starting out as a producer! As soon as I mentioned applying for the job in San Francisco, he offered to call the news director (again, on her personal cell phone) and sang my praises. For that, I'll never be more grateful. Channel your inner reporter by scouring LinkedIn, social media, and search engines for any and all possible connections.

REJECTION CAN BE AWESOME . . . EVENTUALLY

Whether breaking up with a high school sweetheart after 10 years or being passed over for a big job, I get rejection. Second only to actors in Hollywood, I've probably been rejected more times than the average human being. Not just for jobs, but on a daily basis by sources or man-on-the-street interviews. (What do you mean you don't want to weigh in on the current political climate for the entire world to see?!)

Nearly every time I've gotten a "no," something better happens. Instead of seeing a rejection as a negative, let's change the meaning to make it a kick-in-the-pants motivator to keep pushing for something better.

Graciousness in Acceptance . . . and Rejection (The Cruffins)

As soon as I woke up the day after my job interview in San Francisco, I got in line at one of the hottest bakeries in the city: Mr. Holmes Bakehouse. After standing in line long enough for my calves to ache, I practically cleared them out of their signature hipster muffin–croissants, called "Cruffins," before they sold out for the day. (For a while, sweet tooths would actually *hire* people via TaskRabbit or Craigslist to wait in line early in the morning to secure their servings of flaky goodness. That's how in demand they were!) Those two beautiful gold-foil-embossed boxes of hard-to-get, Instagram-worthy pastries cost at least four times the price of Krispy Kreme, but I wanted to make an impression—a sweet, thoughtful impression that not only screamed exclusivity but showed my appreciation for everyone taking time out of their day to interview me. Yes, my future teammates were worth the $4 per Cruffin and the wait in line

The treats were a hit. Even the general manager wrote a note to say how much everyone loved the surprise. (Scientists do say sugar is more addictive than cocaine. Maybe I had somehow drugged them into euphoria.) Shortly after, I got the job.

While I wouldn't recommend going to these lengths for every interview (A friend once asked if she should send a cheese pizza after a phone interview. Uh, the answer there is a resounding *no*.) and I certainly wouldn't recommend this after not getting the job, there are certain measures that ooze gratitude, appreciation, and class and set you up for . . . who knows? Maybe something even better the next time around.

- **Make It Memorable:** Would I have made the same impression with stale Dunkin' Donuts as I did with artisan-crafted non-GMO/organic/locally sourced pastry? Probably not. So, the same applies for after you get rejected. A nice card (preferably not the 99-cent cheap-o cards at the bottom of the Hallmark display) with a message that reads something like, "Thank you for the opportunity to interview for your position. While I'm disappointed it didn't work out, please keep me in mind for the next one." And add a personal tidbit to the end. When I didn't get a job in Dallas, I included a line that said, "Next time, I'm getting the baby back ribs!" a play on the pathetic and too-healthy salad I ordered at the BBQ joint we went to for my interview dinner. Years later, when I ran into that manager at a convention, one of her first questions was if I had made the right choice at the hotel breakfast buffet.

- **Continue to Follow Up:** Even though I didn't get the job in Boston . . . or DC . . . or Philadelphia and I don't want the jobs now, I still, on occasion, take the time to email the news directors or various managers during holiday time to let them know what I'm up to and to wish them season's greetings. November and December make for the perfect built-in excuse to connect. Because the gesture is a positive one, and one where you're not asking for something, you come across as genuine and kind, not desperate as if you need a job. It also leaves a positive message with the employer to remember you for the next round of hiring . . . just in case.

THE EVERYDAY F**K UPS

Screwing up sucks. Screwing up in front of the boss and hundreds of thousands of viewers is a whole different beast, and it used to eat me up inside until I couldn't sleep and developed that subconscious jaw-grinding problem.

The goal is to train your brain to face a mistake head-on and get through it and not let it affect how others view your work, so you can go on to thrive.

Permit Patty: A Case for 'Fessing Up and Moving On

Let's face it. No matter how good you are at your job, how careful you are in crossing every "t" and dotting every "i," you're bound to make a mistake. A faux pas. A snafu. A momentary lapse in judgment. Whatever you call your f**k up, how you respond to it can be the difference between making a full recovery and going on to thrive, or having a black mark on your record, being on a never-ending mental treadmill reliving what went wrong, or potentially losing your job. As much as we'd like to have our own personal Olivia Pope clean up our scandals and missteps in our careers, the only person who can fill that role in real life is you.

In the summer of 2018, America was experiencing a news phenomenon. People, behaving badly, perhaps in a racially charged way, were being caught on camera. The videos would go viral, racking up millions of views, shares, and even more rage-filled comments. Accompanying the viral videos, Instagram posts and stories would be an alliteration nickname. "Coupon Carl" in Chicago, for calling the cops on a black woman, accusing her of trying to use an expired voucher for incontinence pads. "Barbecue Becky," who called the police on a group of African American people grilling at a lake in Oakland, California. "Pool Patrol Paula," who was caught hitting a black teen, calling her the "n" word, and then biting the responding officer. Yeesh, was this the zombie apocalypse or something?

Then, there was "Permit Patty."

My photographer and I were staked outside a condo complex across the street from the Giants stadium, where a woman known to the world as "Permit Patty" was holed up. She was at the epicenter of the latest viral video scandal to circle the globe—a white woman, caught on camera, appearing to report an eight-year-old black girl for selling water on the street outside her home without a permit. The story spread like wildfire. The original Instagram video (complete with funny expletive) depicting the woman seemingly hiding from the little girl's mother and calling the police has been viewed millions of times to date. (Patty was adamant she did not call the police. It just "appeared" that way in the video.) Forget about the immigration crisis and the thousands of crying children separated at the border. Whatever the reason, the universe just couldn't get enough of Miss Patty.

Since the incident happened less than 10 minutes from my station, I was determined to be the first local reporter to score an interview with her. After some persistent reaching out (in my world, that includes at least five phone calls and an equal amount of texts), Permit Patty's representative finally texted me back. The message read, in part, that his client was "traumatized," and didn't want to do any more on-camera interviews.

Yes! Even though he declined my request, it was an in. As you know from this book, once you find the "in"—it's usually all downhill from there. One thing I'm known for is a pretty good success rate turning the "in" into an "in-terview."

So it began. Back and forth. Back and forth. I was starting to develop carpal tunnel in my thumbs from frantically texting and trying to get this "PR expert" to understand my reasoning why his client should grant me an interview. I explained how, if his client was "traumatized" now, she'd be a whole lot more traumatized if the story kept growing. Speaking out was her chance to tell her side of the story. A chance at the world to empathize with her situation. Control the narrative and be in control of the story. It felt as if I was getting close. Mr. PR said to "hold on" and I anxiously held on with bated breath. This was going to be awesome! I would have the biggest story of the day.

Twenty minutes of "holding on" later, I watched in disgust as the CNN reporter cockily signaled to his cameraperson and strode into her building. *Seriously!?* The only logical conclusion was they signed a pay-for-play deal, which included a gag clause where she wouldn't be able to talk to any other media outlet.

Grrr. After working the story for hours, wasting my time with Mr. PR Genius, and I get a silent slap in the face? It wasn't exactly a good day. As I resisted the urge to broadcast what just happened all over Twitter, and thought about the snub well after I went home from work, I took comfort in knowing soon enough that Patty's PR guru would understand my point: by not putting the story to bed, it was about to get a whole lot messier for his client.

Lo and behold, not only did the story stay alive, it intensified. Another station, who was also denied an interview, kept digging into Patty's actions that day. Turns out, she did indeed talk to the police, but called 9-1-1 to do so. Calling 9-1-1 isn't the same as calling the police, but from the phone records, you can hear Patty get transferred to the police department. Whether or not she purposely evaded that minor detail didn't matter. She looked even worse in the eyes of millions and ended up resigning from her job as CEO of a medical marijuana company.

You should have listened when you had the chance, PR guy.

NOW. NOT TOMORROW. NOT NEXT WEEK. *NOW* (THE IMPORTANCE OF IMMEDIACY)

The Permit Patty story is a prime example of when an apology is needed; time is of the essence. How many politicians have you seen go down in flames for not 'fessing up to their misdeeds? (Anthony Weiner, we all knew it was you in those topless selfies.) The same goes when the blame is on you. By not acting quickly, you're giving the impression you don't care. The quicker you can take care of the situation, the quicker others will get over it and the quicker you can get on with your life.

Here's my three-step process to contain a faux pas, and move on with professionalism and as little damage to your reputation and career as possible.

Own It!

C'mon. Be honest! Are you really at fault? If you are, then you are! Shifting the blame to someone else just makes the situation worse, because you look like a wimp, someone else gets thrown under the bus, and the mess-up then continues to grow. If someone else is responsible in addition to yourself, mention it, but you're an adult: take the heat for your own actions. Oh, and don't lie or lie by omission. It's amazing how easily someone can find out the truth.

Apologize Sincerely and Succinctly

Don't say more than you need to! A reporter I used to work with would get nervous and start rambling during his apologies. So much so I started feeling badly for him and had to pull him aside and give him a talk on why he was digging his own grave the more he rambled. Plus, your job isn't to keep reminding others of your blunders; it's to get past them.

Work Your Butt Off

Regaining your team's trust after a gaffe takes a whole lot longer than proving yourself in the first place. Just like a cheating spouse lavishing his or her partner with flowers, gifts, and lovey-dovey pet names after getting caught in the act, you have to work twice as hard to prove yourself. The only thing that erases a mistake is an overabundance of stellar work, and nobody can take that away from you.

WHAT THE FUTURE HOLDS

As much as I'd like to wrap this chapter up in a neat little bow, let's get one thing straight: career setbacks are never fun. From the unintentional mistakes to the unfortunate developments at your job that result in something that is beyond your control like being let go, these create inconvenient, stressful, and sometimes embarrassing and heartbreaking times.

To an outsider, looking back at that time of transition from one Bay Area to another, many things don't look right on paper. The cost of living in San Francisco is astronomical (It's the most expensive city in the country, with the average home price at

$1,300 a square foot. Tampa Bay was $200.), yet I'm not making more money. I'm no longer the face of a television station. I work weekends and more hours than I ever imagined were possible.

But at the same time, it takes being pushed out of something cushy and comfortable to realize your full potential and find true joy. Being back on the street reporting shouldn't have been seen as a career demotion. It was an opportunity to meet seemingly ordinary people who accomplished extraordinary things. It was exciting and energizing and helped me remember why I got into the industry to begin with: to help others by telling their story. Sure, living the Florida life of leisure, state income–tax-free, toes in warm sand and surf was good. But it turns out, coasting wasn't for me. A setback can reignite passions and drive and force you to create opportunities for yourself that'll make you feel alive. For me, I'm alive for the first time in my career and in my personal life. The adventure to new surroundings is better than anything I dared to dream of back in Florida. A former mentor had a saying: You've never really lived until you've been fired. When you're in the moment where it feels like the world is caving in, don't forget that feeling of fulfillment is just beyond the horizon and may not happen until you decide to fail your way forward.

Epilogue

TWO WEEKS BEFORE this manuscript was due to my publisher, I was feeling confident and excited to be one step closer to sharing my career experiences and work-life lessons with the universe. Sold-out book tours, signings, and *New York Times* Best Sellers List, here I come!

Then, I had an unexpected communication meltdown.

One hour before being live on the scene of a traffic nightmare so bad it was deemed #carmageddon, I was paired with the only photographer I ever purposely dodged. The one bump in my workplace yellow brick road that made an otherwise smooth and pleasant work-life torturous. The last thing I wanted to do was be trapped in a live van with this photographer for the next nine hours, trying to play nice while ignoring his disparaging remarks about women and laziness.

On this day, I had enough.

Frustrated, angry tears unexpectedly started welling in my eyes and I excused myself from the newsroom. How could this be happening!? I just wrote a 70,000-word book on communication and here I was, hiding out in a dark edit room until I could calm my breathing enough to face the world and begin my assignment.

As I gasped for air, on the brink of hyperventilating, I realized something. I had done everything right and the best I could up until this point, and I wasn't going to let another human being take away my dignity like this. This visceral reaction was a beacon that this situation needed to escalate to the next level. Two fellow female reporters, close to my age, told me in confidence several months earlier that they had the same experiences and also tried to avoid the photographer at all costs.

With red-rimmed eyes, I pulled a manager to the side and said, "Walk with me." We made it to a nearby stairwell and as best I could I laid out the issue at hand as concisely and cohesively as possible using everything I had learned along the way in my five-city journey to be sure my message was getting across clearly and was taken seriously. It was. Less than five minutes later, I was re-assigned to another photographer (who was known for his professionalism and hard work) and we hit the ground running going live multiple times throughout the night, kicking butt the best we knew how.

The truth is, when you have a record and a reputation for effectively communicating more than 99.9 percent of the time, you have the luxury of credibility. You are allowed to have a momentary lapse to process and strategize your next move. Even if you effectively accomplish everything in this book, it's not always going to be roses, unicorns, and bluebirds landing on your outstretched finger. You can't control how other people behave, act, or carry themselves. But if you're able to apply bits and pieces of the techniques discussed every so often and get through something you otherwise wouldn't have another day—take the small victory. Use that as training ground for tackling the next situation.

Index

A

ABC World News Tonight, 116
Accepting yourself, 177–181
Acton School of Business, 118
Ad-libbing, 127–134
Adults, as giant children, 172–173
Advice, unwelcome, 65–66
Age, chronological, 173–176
ALS Ice Bucket Challenge, 12–14
Always being ready, 188–191
Anchorman (film), 32, 48
Answer, letting others, 155–156
Anticipating others' needs, 190–191
Apologies:
    avoiding, in Gloss and Go, 34
    expressing regret as alternative to,
      39–40
    with follow-ups, 121
    genuine, 40
    sincere and succinct, 225
Appropriate asking, 148
Ask:
    power of the, 145–150
    showcasing your, 156–159

Asking for what you want, 151–156
Attacks, responding to, 180
Attention, capturing someone's,
    124–126
Attire, appropriate, 193–197
Audience, hooking the, 126–127
Available, being, 191
Awards, 170

B

Backgrounds, researching others',
    115–118, 218
"Be right back," 122–124
Believing in yourself, 161–186
    by accepting yourself, 177–181
    and chronological age, 173–176
    by empowering others, 181–182
    by laughing at yourself, 171–173
    by letting yourself be empowered
      by others, 182–186
    by making your own name, 163–167
    by not comparing yourself to
      others, 169–171
    by overcoming doubt, 167–169

Bermuda Triangle, social, 27–28

Best Buddies, 123

"Best," subjectivity of, 169–171

Betta fish, 47–48

Blunt, being, 10–12, 36–39

Body shaming, 88–90

Bodyguards, 48

Boehner, John, 165, 169

Bold statement, making a, 126

Bonds, Barry, 147

Bornstein, Helen, 10

Bornstein, Marc, 10

Branding, 166

Broadcasting and Cable (journal), 200

Brokaw, Tom, 209

The brushoff, 56

Bullying, 64–66

Bureau of Labor Statistics, 200

Business cards, 143

C

Career setbacks, 199–226
  anticipating, 203–204
  and changing your perspective, 211–213
  and dealing with mistakes, 221–224
  and dodging the bullet, 213–215
  and the future, 225–226
  layoffs as, 204–209
  and new opportunities, 216–218
  preparing for, 200–203
  and rejection, 218–221
  responding immediately to, 224–225

Carr Fire, 151–153

Catch Me If You Can (film), 98

Celebrities, overcoming fear of, 118–120

Challenges, deciding not to respond to, 21

Charlotte, N.C., 128, 212

Chronological age, 173–176

Chung, Connie, 164

Cocking of the head, 9

Coffee, meeting for, 150

Comparing yourself to others, 169–171

Competitiveness, 48

Complainers, 40–42

Compliments, 104–106

Connecting with others, 143–159
  and asking for what you want, 151–156
  and finding "hidden gems," 144–145
  and power of the ask, 145–150
  and showcasing your ask, 156–159

Contacts, keeping up with, 149–150

Control, 3–4

Conversation(s):
  being left out of, 27–28
  getting out of interminable, 11–12
  responding to upsetting, 7
  steering the, 140–141
  (*See also* Survival speak)

Conversation starters, 101–102

Convictions, sticking to your, 86–87

Core group, having a, 208–209

Corpse flower, 157–159

Coworkers:
  competition by, 48
  personal data mining by, 53–55
  prying by, 52–57

Craigslist, 219

Crazy Rich Asians (film), 22

Cronkite, Walter, 164
Crying, 7–8

D

Data mining, personal, 53–55
Debates, avoiding, 181
Decision making, 74
Deflecting, 34–35
Democratic National Convention, 128–129, 157
Details, describing the, 131–134
DiCaprio, Leonardo, 98
Digestibility, of feedback, 73
Direct, being, 12
Discussion, fostering, 181
Dodging the bullet, 213–215
Doubt, overcoming, 167–169
Downs, Hugh, 32
"Dress for the job you want," 189
Drifting eyes, 9
Dumbledore (character), 64

E

East Coasters, 10
Ego, stroking someone's, 35–36
Emails, reacting to upsetting, 6–7
Emerson College, 109
Emotion:
  power of, when reacting, 3–7
  showing, 7–8
Empathy:
  listening with, 110
  showing, 42
Empowerment:
  by others, 182–186
  of others, 181–182
Engaged:
  avoiding being, 121
  staying, 108–114

Enraged people, dealing with, 34
Equals, treating others as, 145
Escobar, Pablo, 121
The everywhere ask, 148
Examples, following feedback with, 73–74
Excuses, for making a graceful exit, 121
Extra attention, avoiding, 168
Eye contact:
  with audience, 127
  maintaining, 111–113
  as visual cue, 8–9

F

Facebook, 62, 67, 75, 119, 150, 152, 158, 162, 172
Facts:
  backing up with, 180–181
  sticking to the, 92
Feedback:
  getting, 66–72
  giving, 72–75
Feeling, showing, 7–8
Feeling sorry for yourself, 207
Feigning ignorance, 56
Ferrell, Will, 32
Firm, being, 56–57
Follow-ups, when making a graceful exit, 121
Forbes magazine, 118
Ford, Christine Blasey, 83–84, 187
"Forgive and forget," 24
Forgiveness, asking for, 130–131
Frank Abagnale, Jr. (character), 98
Friends, making, 60–64
Frowning, 9
F**k ups, everyday, 221–224

G

"Getting goodies back," 63–64
Getting to the point, 127
Getting what you want, 42–46
Glamour magazine, 70, 192
Glazed-over eyes, 9
Gloss and Go, 31–35
Go-bags, 189
Golden State Warriors, 177, 181
Google, 133
Graceful exit, making a, 120–124
Groups:
    core, 208–209
    professional, 61–64

H

Handshakes, 107
Happy, finding what makes you,
    166–167
Hazing periods, 49–50
"Hey, can I ask you a question?"
    approach, 102
"Hidden gems," finding, 144–145
Hooking the audience, 126–127
HR, sexual harassment and going to,
    90–92
Huffington, Arianna, 129
Humor, using, 29–31
Hurston, Zora Neale, 61

I

#IBelieveChristine, 84
Ignorance, feigning, 56
Immediacy, importance of, 224–225
"In," finding an, 101–102
Instagram, 136, 152, 158, 172, 222
Interviewing, using silence when,
    113–114

Intuition, using your, 203–204
Iwu, Adama, 79

J

Jennings, Peter, 209
John J. Heldrich Center for
    Workforce Development
    (Rutgers), 204
Joking, 29–31

K

Kavanaugh, Brett, 43, 45, 83–84
Kilauea volcano, 88
Knee-jerk reactions, 6–7, 19
Kondo, Marie, 216
Kosciusko, Miss., 217

L

Laughing at yourself, 171–173
Laughter, 29–31
Layoffs:
    being prepared for, 200–203
    dealing with, 204–209
Leader, your inner, 5–6
Lee, Ed, 146–147
Left out, being, 27–28
Lim, Evan, 22
LinkedIn, 202, 210
Listening:
    with empathy, 110
    encouraging, in others,
        124–127
"Listening window," 125
Look, finding your, 192–193
Lowest common denominator,
    finding the, 28–29

M

Making your own name, 163–167
Mantou, 99
Memorable, staying, 106–108
Mental inventories, 179
#MeToo, 79, 91
Microsoft, 124
Midland, Mich., 99
Milano, Alyssa, 79
Minaj, Nicki, 49–50
Mirroring, 117–118
Mistakes:
 addressing, 131, 134–136
 avoiding drawing extra attention
  to, 168
 dealing with, 221–224
 owning your, 224
 steamrolling over, 168–169
Montana, Joe, 147
Motives, ulterior, 50–52
Mr. Holmes Bakehouse (San
  Francisco), 219
MSNBC, 129
Murrow, Edward R., 32

N

Name, making your own, 163–167
National Association of Black
  Journalists (NABJ), 106
Needs, anticipating others',
  190–191
Netflix, 216
Networking, 149–150, 202 (*See also*
  Connecting with others)
New York Times, 79, 187
"No offense," 17–18
The non-ask ask, 156
Nonvisual memory making, 107

Nooyi, Indra, 93
Notes, sending, 149–150

O

Obama, Michelle, 157
Obvious, stating the, 102–106
Offended, being, 17–18
Off-the-cuff remarks, making,
  127–134
Opportunities, embracing new,
  216–218
Oscars, 98, 135
Over-complainers, 92
Owning your mistakes, 224

P

Passion, showing, 7–8
Pepsi, 93
Perez, Janete, 79
"Person on the street" sound bites,
  102
Personal appearance, 187–197
 and always being ready, 188–191
 and appropriate attire, 193–197
 and finding your look, 192–193
*The Personality and Social Psychology
  Bulletin*, 61
Pet names, 93–95
Philadelphia, Pa., 213–214
Phony compliments, 104, 105
Pity Parties, 184, 207
Positive:
 focusing on the, 213
 reinforcing the, 155–159
Prepared, being, 44–45, 169,
  200–203
Problem solving, steps for, 44–46
Professional groups, 61–64

Proof of performance, 156
Prying, by coworkers, 52–57
Public speaking:
  fear of, 129
  screw-ups when, 134–136
Punctual, being, 191
Purposeful asking, 147–148

Q

Quick responses, 136–139
Quirks, memorable, 107–108

R

Ramblers, 108–109, 113–114
Rather, Dan, 106–107, 209–211
Reacting, 1–24
  by being blunt, 10–12
  and eye contact, 8–9
  knee-jerk reactions, 6–7, 19
  and power of reactions, 3–7
  and power of silence, 18–24
  in "real life," 15–17
  and recognizing others' reactions, 4
  and regretting reactions, 12–18
  showing passion and feeling when,
    7–8
  and stepping back, 14
  visual cues when, 8–10
  when offended, 17–18
  to yelling, 19–21
Ready, always being, 188–191
Ready retorts, 136–139
Regret:
  expressing, 39–40
  reaction, 12–18
Rehearsing, 130
Rejection, 218–221
Relief, from being direct, 39
Respecting others, 179–180

Ron Burgundy (character), 32, 48
Rutgers University, 204

S

San Francisco, Calif., 146–147,
  225–226
Sandwich technique, 155
Self-control, 4
Self-depreciation, 171–173
Setbacks, career (*see* Career setbacks)
Severe weather, covering, 194–196
Sexism, 87
Sexual harassment, 77–95
  escalating the response to, 83–87
  pet names as form of, 93–95
  and standing up for yourself and
    others, 87–90
  step-wise response to, 79–83
  and when to go to HR, 90–92
Shifting eyes, 9
Side chat, mastering the, 28–29
Side hustling, 202–203
Sign-offs, anchor, 31–33
Silence:
  calculated, 21–24
  power of, 18–24
  using, when interviewing,
    113–114
"Simon" (game), 111
Skirting, 42
Smiling, 104
Social Bermuda Triangle, 27–28
Social media, maintaining
  relationships via, 150
Socializing, overcoming fear of,
  99–101
Solution, proposing a, 156
Standing up for yourself and others,
  87–90

Staying engaged, 108–114
Staying on topic, 86
Steering the conversation, 140–141
Stepping back, 14
Stop Street Harassment, 78
Storytelling, 4
Surroundings, getting a feel for your, 103–104
Survival speak, 97–141
  and ad-libbing, 127–134
  and finding an "in," 101–102
  and getting others to listen, 124–127
  and handling public-speaking screw-ups, 134–136
  and making a graceful exit, 120–124
  and overcoming fear of celebrities, 118–120
  and overcoming fear of socializing, 99–101
  and researching others' backgrounds, 115–118
  and responding to "what do you do?," 139
  and stating the obvious, 102–106
  and staying engaged, 108–114
  and staying memorable, 106–108
  and steering the conversation, 140–141
  and using ready retorts, 136–139

T

Tabloids, 126
TaskRabbit, 219
Teleprompters, 129–130
Testing the waters, 57–60
"Thank you," as response to compliments, 104, 106

Thinking, reacting without, 6
Thousand Oaks, Calif., 154
Tiger Moms, 37, 163
Time, precious nature of, 121
Time magazine, 147
Timing, 191, 224–225
Tone matching, 83
Toxic relationships, 183–186
Traits, memorable, 107–108
Trust, learning to, 57–60
Twitter, 79, 152, 172, 181

U

"Uhms," avoiding, 127
Ulterior motives, 50–52
University of California, Berkeley, 187
University of Cambridge, 146
Unresolved issues, handling, 16–17

V

Vague answers, giving, 55
"Verbal vortex," 11
Viral videos, racially-charged, 221–224
Visual cues, 8–10

W

Walking speed, 10
Watching your back, 47–75
  and bullying by others, 64–66
  and getting feedback, 66–72
  and giving feedback, 72–75
  and learning to trust, 57–60
  and making friends, 60–64
  with prying coworkers, 52–57
  and surviving the hazing period, 49–50
  and ulterior motives, 50–52
Weinstein, Harvey, 79

"What do you do?," responding to, 139
What you want, getting, 42–46
Whiners, 40–42
will.i.am, 147
Winfrey, Oprah, 24, 72, 217
Women in the World, 93
Women's March (San Francisco),
  79, 147

Woodruff, Bob, 115–116
Work samples, keeping, 201–202

Y

Yelling, 19–21
Yourself, believing in (*see* Believing
  in yourself)
YouTube, 132–133, 201

About the Author

*D*ION LIM is an Emmy Award–winning TV news anchor and reporter at ABC in San Francisco. She has traveled the country covering everything from devastating wildfires to celebrities on the red carpet at the Oscars, and the landmark Brett Kavanaugh hearing in Washington, DC to the Warriors champagne locker room celebration at the NBA championships.

Dion has been featured in publications ranging from *Glamour* to *The Daily Mail* and her writing has appeared online for the *Huffington Post* and in Amy Poehler's *Smart Girls*. A sought-after speaker known for her candor and engaging style, Dion has hosted and emceed events alongside Hollywood A-Listers like Patrick Dempsey to tech-titan Guy Kawasaki and news legend Dan Rather. Dion is also heavily involved in workshops and key-noting for professional development groups, including the Asian American Journalists Association and Ascend Leadership, which is the largest nonprofit Pan-Asian organization for professionals in North America. She was recently named the Bay Area's Champion of the Year for the nonprofit Best Buddies, for her involvement in championing the cause of inclusivity for those with intellectual and developmental disabilities.

Prior to being in the Bay Area, Dion worked every shift imaginable, climbing the competitive TV news ladder. She spent time as a reporter and worked the morning, afternoon, early evening, and primary anchor positions in Massachusetts, Kansas City, Charlotte, and Tampa Bay. While Dion doesn't believe success is measured only in awards, she is proud to say she has been named by various publications as "Best Morning News Anchor" and "Best TV Personality."

Dion's love of storytelling started at a young age. The daughter of Chinese immigrants who, instead of watching cartoons, encouraged her to learn "proper English" by watching TV news anchors. When she realized her parents' desired destiny for her to become a doctor, lawyer, or scientist wouldn't pan out due to her stunningly mediocre test scores and GPA, she begged the high school journalism teacher to accept her into senior-level television classes, where she could talk and write (instead of do math) and the rest is history.

She and her husband, a professional poker player, live in San Francisco and share a love of travel, discovering great food, and Dachshunds. You can keep up with Dion on Facebook, Instagram, and Twitter @DionLimTV and at www.dionlim.com.